Brigitta Schwartz

Social Isolation Resulting from Stigma in Dementia

Brigitta Schwartz

Social Isolation Resulting from Stigma in Dementia

LAP LAMBERT Academic Publishing

Impressum/Imprint (nur für Deutschland/ only for Germany)
Bibliografische Information der Deutschen Nationalbibliothek: Die Deutsche Nationalbibliothek verzeichnet diese Publikation in der Deutschen Nationalbibliografie; detaillierte bibliografische Daten sind im Internet über http://dnb.d-nb.de abrufbar.

Alle in diesem Buch genannten Marken und Produktnamen unterliegen warenzeichen-, marken- oder patentrechtlichem Schutz bzw. sind Warenzeichen oder eingetragene Warenzeichen der jeweiligen Inhaber. Die Wiedergabe von Marken, Produktnamen, Gebrauchsnamen, Handelsnamen, Warenbezeichnungen u.s.w. in diesem Werk berechtigt auch ohne besondere Kennzeichnung nicht zu der Annahme, dass solche Namen im Sinne der Warenzeichen- und Markenschutzgesetzgebung als frei zu betrachten wären und daher von jedermann benutzt werden dürften.

Coverbild: www.ingimage.com

Verlag: LAP LAMBERT Academic Publishing AG & Co. KG
Dudweiler Landstr. 99, 66123 Saarbrücken, Deutschland
Telefon +49 681 3720-310, Telefax +49 681 3720-3109
Email: info@lap-publishing.com

Herstellung in Deutschland:
Schaltungsdienst Lange o.H.G., Berlin
Books on Demand GmbH, Norderstedt
Reha GmbH, Saarbrücken
Amazon Distribution GmbH, Leipzig
ISBN: 978-3-8383-8005-6

Imprint (only for USA, GB)
Bibliographic information published by the Deutsche Nationalbibliothek: The Deutsche Nationalbibliothek lists this publication in the Deutsche Nationalbibliografie; detailed bibliographic data are available in the Internet at http://dnb.d-nb.de.

Any brand names and product names mentioned in this book are subject to trademark, brand or patent protection and are trademarks or registered trademarks of their respective holders. The use of brand names, product names, common names, trade names, product descriptions etc. even without a particular marking in this works is in no way to be construed to mean that such names may be regarded as unrestricted in respect of trademark and brand protection legislation and could thus be used by anyone.

Cover image: www.ingimage.com

Publisher: LAP LAMBERT Academic Publishing AG & Co. KG
Dudweiler Landstr. 99, 66123 Saarbrücken, Germany
Phone +49 681 3720-310, Fax +49 681 3720-3109
Email: info@lap-publishing.com

Printed in the U.S.A.
Printed in the U.K. by (see last page)
ISBN: 978-3-8383-8005-6

Copyright © 2010 by the author and LAP LAMBERT Academic Publishing AG & Co. KG and licensors
All rights reserved. Saarbrücken 2010

Contents

Contents..ii

1. Introduction 1
1.1 Ageing Population
1.2 Disability
1.3 Dementia
1.4 Stigma
1.6 What is Stigma?
1.7 Labeling and Stereotyping
1.8 Separation
1.9 Status Loss
1.10 Stigma in Dementia
1.11 Social isolation of pwd and their carers
1.12 Stigma of Ageism
1.13 Use It or Lose It – Risk Factors for Dementia
1.14 Change in Social Support

2. The Present Study..21
2.1 Aims and Rationale
2.2 Hypotheses

3. Method..24
3.1 Participants
3.2 Measures
3.3 Social Embeddedness
3.4 Received and provided support
3.5 Perceived Satisfaction with Support
3.6 Procedure
3.7 Data Analysis

4. Results..30
4.1 Reliability Analyses for each Measure of Social Support
4.2 Social Embeddedness
4.3 Received and provided support
4.4 Perceived Satisfaction with Support
4.5 Significant changes in social support for the Australian carers of pwd.
4.6 Comparing Australian and US samples
4.7 Correlations
4.8 Alzheimers, Cardiovascular dementia and Other dementias
4.9 Early- Mid and Late stages of dementia
4.10 New Friends or No New Friends

5. Discussion...48
5.1 Comparisons of Australian carers of pwd with US healthy older population
5.2 Negative interactions
5.3 Alzheimers, Cardiovascular and Other types of dementia
5.4 Early, Mid and Late stages of dementia
5.5 New friends made or no friends made
5.6 Implications for interventions
5.7 Suggestions
5.8 Limitations of the present study
5.9 Conclusion

References...67

Appendix A – Ethics approval

Appendix B – Information Letter

Appendix C – Tables
Table 1 Comparisons US and Australian samples
Table 2 Comparisons Alz, Cardio and Other
Table 3 Comparison Early, Mid and Late
Table 4 Comparison Newfriends and Nofriends

Appendix D – Adapted Social Support Questionnaire

Social Isolation Resulting from Stigma in Dementia

Ageing Population

As the ageing part of the population seems to be expanding, issues related to older adults are becoming more and more important. The baby boomers are advancing to retirement, and the population of older people will soon reach unprecedented numbers (Longino, 2005).
The Australian Bureau of Statistics (ABS) conducted a survey of Disability, Ageing and Care (SDAC) throughout Australia. This survey found that the population of older people had risen by one percent between 1998 and 2003, from 16% to 17% of the total population (ABS, 2003). The Australian Institute of Health and Welfare (AIHW) have projected that the older proportion of the population will climb to 20% in 2024. The fastest growing part of the population are the oldest old, people over 85 (AIHW, 2006).

Disability

Just over half of these people (51%) had a reported disability, and 19% had a profound or severe core-activity limitation. A core activity is an activity of daily living, and part of the activities a person needs to be able to perform daily in areas of personal self-care and generally around their own home, to function independently. Twenty-six percent of people between 60 and 69 years reported the need for assistance, yet in the over 85 year range, 84% of people had a need for assistance, which represents a much higher percentage (ABS, 2003).
In 2003, there were 2.6 million carers in Australia. Over half of the people who provide care to people who are older and/or have a disability are women. Nearly a fifth of all carers are primary carers, the person who provides most of the informal help to a person with a disability. Most of these primary carers are 35-54 year old women (71%), caring for ageing parents, children and partners. Twenty-

four percent of primary carers are over 65 years of age, and caring primarily for a partner. This is nearly double the rate than for the rest of the population (ABS, 2003)

Most people with a disability had physical problems (84%). The remaining 16% had a mental or behavioural disorder as their main problem. However, those people whose main condition was a mental or behavioural disorder were more likely to have a profound or severe core-activity limitation than those with a physical condition (46% compared to 29%). Fifty-two percent of women aged 80 years and over had a profound or severe core-activity limitation, whereas only 34% of men of the same age had such a severe limitation (ABS, 2003).
When people are severely limited in core activities of self-care, mobility or communication, they are said to be profoundly or severely limited in their activities of daily living, and are dependent on their carers for most or all activities of daily living, placing considerable strain on those who care for them (ABS, 2003; AIHW, 2006).
Over half (56%) of people with mental or behavioural disorders, such as dementia and depression, had a profound or severe core-activity limitation. This compares to 33% for physical conditions with the highest rates of profound or severe core-activity limitation, being for heart disease or diseases of the nervous system.

Dementia

People over the age of 65 are twice as likely to be diagnosed with dementia than younger people, and this risk doubles again every further five years of life, until dementia affects 24% of people over the age of 85 (AIHW, 2006). In other words, the average rate of moderate to severe dementia amongst Australians is about one in fifteen aged over 65 years of age; among people aged 80 to 84 the rate is one in nine, and among those aged over 85 it is one in four (Alzheimers Australia, 2005).

Thus, the increase of the older and especially the projected doubling of the oldest population means that there will be many more people diagnosed with dementia in the years to come (AIHW, 2006; Alzheimers Australia, 2005; ABS, 2003)

It seems that older adults are facing more problems than were imagined before this population explosion of older people: dementia has grown to be a major problem for this section of the community, and a major factor in health care provision. The impact of dementia on all people who are affected directly, either as the person with dementia (pwd) or the carer for the person, is extensive (Nolan, McCarron, McCallion & Murphy-Lawless, 2006).

Dementia is the term used to describe the symptoms of a large group of illnesses, which cause a progressive decline in a person's mental functioning. It is a broad term, which describes a loss of memory, intellect, rationality, social skills and normal emotional reactions (Alzheimers Australia, 2005; AIHW, 2006) The most prevalent type of dementia is Alzheimers Disease, about 65% of pwd are affected by this illness; the second largest group is Cardiovascular Dementia, around 25% of pwd are diagnosed with this illness; around 10% of pwd are affected by a range of illnesses such as Dementia with Lewy Bodies, Fronto-Temporal Dementia, Pick's Disease and approximately another hundred more unusual dementias (Alzheimers Australia, 2005).

Currently in Australia, there are 227,300 people with dementia, with the number expected to be 731,000 by 2050 unless there is a medical breakthrough. Dementia affects the lives of nearly one million Australians who are involved in caring for a family member or friend with dementia. By 2016, dementia will be the largest source of disability burden. Between 2000 and 2050, the number of people with dementia in Australia is expected to increase by 327%, while the total population increases by less than 40%. Worldwide, there are currently 29.8 million people with dementia, with the number expected to be 81.1 million by 2050 (AIHW, 2006; Alzheimers Australia, 2005; Cummings & Benson, 2003).

Stigma

A person, who is afflicted by a chronic illness or disability such as dementia, can be perceived as different from the general population and that could subject this individual to possible stigmatisation and discrimination by others who do not have the disability (Nolan et. al., 2006). Unfortunately dementia, as a mentally disabling condition, is associated with stigma, and that means that people with dementia and their carers are not only having to deal with losses of abilities and the consequences arising from these losses, they are also exposed to the outcomes of stigma.

Different cultures deal with the stigma of dementia in different ways.
Some cultures hide the illness, as for example Polish culture, for reasons pertaining to the horror of war experiences regarding the extermination of defective individuals. South Asians do not want to diminish the marriage prospects of their young people through having a mental illness in the family. South Asians may also be concerned about the religious and magical properties of dementia, pertaining to punishment for a previous life (Mackenzie, 2006). –

Some cultures such as the Chinese, tend to deny that there is any problem with the mind of the person with dementia, by stating that forgetfulness is a normal part of ageing. The Chinese further believe that any research into dementia, involving the pwd personally, will only worry the pwd needlessly without giving any benefits (Hinton et al, 2000). In Portugal, people with dementia are given medications but the dementia label is avoided for reasons of exemption from nursing home care (Iliffe, et al, 2003).
Most of the ways of dealing with the person with dementia in Ireland are, as Nolan (2006) stated, centred around "a dark secret". Lack of awareness of dementia amongst older citizens seems a function of a limited concept of the disability that includes only its more advanced features. Often general practitioners have limited exposure to dementia, and their embarrassment of

discussing memory loss, functional losses and incontinence, and their reluctance to damage long standing relationships with their patients, act as obstacles to the recognition of dementia (Iliffe et al, 2003).

In the U.K., stigma is a concern in dementia care provision and an obstacle to well-being and quality of life. For example, stigma has been shown to impact on delays in dementia recognition by family members, who try to disguise changes in the person with dementia (pwd) as 'part of normal ageing', until a crisis occurs. Thus, diagnosis and primary care, as well as supportive services are delayed to the point where the carer might also become ill due to unresolved problems and stress, compounding the previous problems (Benbow & Reynolds, 2000).

Other cultures have more openness towards the condition. For example, cultures such as The Netherlands or Belgium may be open about the disability and advertise the dementia label as part of a neon light sign over the door of an Alzheimer's Café, as part of a therapeutic approach to accept and welcome pwd into the community of 'café society' and to eradicate the 'us and them' mentality at least to a degree (Iliffe et al, 2003).

As is evident from the above, the way in which dementia is perceived, can have a severe impact on the functioning of both pwd and their carers. In particular denial, hiding or perception of mental deterioration as part of ageing, can disadvantage the person with dementia, as in the early stages medications can be prescribed to improve functioning and delay deterioration for quite some time. People with dementia and carers, who know what lies ahead, can prepare for the future by dealing with the legal and financial implications of the disease. Services, support groups and education can be accessed so families are better equipped to meet the challenges ahead and to avoid the development of crises. It also allows the pwd to have a say in his or her future care and in the making of plans (Manthorpe, 2004). In light of the potentially devastating consequences of stigma for pwd and their carers, the effects of stigma, including social isolation, need to be explored and remediated. As such, this is the focus of the present study.

What is Stigma?

There seem to be many different definitions of stigma, some are linked to aspects of stigma as a 'mark of disgrace' or as the discrimination which results from stigma, and this seems to occur due to the many different circumstances to which the concept can be applied.

Yet, some social scientists challenge the interpretations of the stigma concept and remind us that stigma should be explained from the lived perspectives of the people who are stigmatised (Link & Phelan, 2001; Schneider,1988;). According to Link & Phelan (2001), stigma exists when elements of labelling, stereotyping, separation, status loss and discrimination co-occur against a backdrop of power that allows these processes to occur. Link and Phelan (2001) explain this phenomenon as consisting of components, and start with Goffman's (1963) observation that stigma can be seen as the relationship between an attribute and a stereotype.

Labelling and stereotyping

Labelling people, situations and things is an important and necessary function of our brain, to enable quick identification of categories of people, things and situations in daily life. Categorisation is necessary to enable individuals to deal with people, situations and things quickly. Stereotypes are the result of categorisation, a prototype of a category ready in the mind, as a classification tool (Link and Phelan, 2001).

Most human differences are inconsequential and routinely overlooked, such as the colour of one's umbrella, food preference or hair colour. Other differences, such as skin colour, IQ or religion are extremely salient in some places of the globe, a highly arbitrary social selection of what matters to the society we want to study, at a particular time in history (Link & Phelan, 2001).

Once differences are identified and labelled, they are usually taken for just the way the world is, and hardly questioned at all. There are gay and straight people, blind and sighted people – yet in all categories of people, there might not be a clear demarcation between categories, as is obvious, for example, in skin colours between "black" and "white". Where does black end and white start? And what else influences the definition? This unclear demarcation exposes the arbitrary nature of social labels, and the fact that the differences between people are not located within the people who are labelled, but affixed by society, as the label "witch" was affixed to some women in earlier centuries (Link & Phelan, 2001).

Labels are then linked to stereotypes, to an assortment of negative attributes clustered around the label. People apparently make split second automatic judgements, operating on preconscious levels (Bargh, Chaiken, Govender & Pratto, 1992; Chen & Bargh, 1997).

For example, participants in Link and colleagues' (1987) study used this type of estimation, to determine from vignettes, that mental patients are more dangerous than back-pain patients (Link, Cullen, Frank & Wozniak, 1987).

Positive and negative stereotypes live in the stigmatiser's memory, constructed within the power relations of society, and wait to be activated by a person or by circumstances associated with everyday situations, and also by a person or circumstances associated with stigma (Link & Phelan, 2001,).

Separation

The separation of "us" from "them" is the third feature of stigmatisation, and occurs after the negative stereotypes have been associated with the person. "They" are usually a threat to "us", as "they" are generally lazy, immoral, and a danger to "us" (Link & Phelan, 2001).

The previous processes of labelling, stereotyping and distancing lead to devaluation, rejection and exclusion. This is equivalent to status loss and discrimination, the next stage of the stigma process.

Status Loss

Status loss means a downgrading of the person to a lower place in the status hierarchy, a place that immediately disadvantages the person to lesser outcomes in real life situations: Less influence in group situations, less chance to take the floor and hold it in a meeting, less life chances (Link & Phelan, 2001).
At the point of status loss and discrimination, people deemed 'normal' will deny the stigmatised the life chances that 'normal' people have. A rationale is constructed for devaluing, rejecting and excluding the stigmatised person. This is the point when people become disadvantaged regarding income, education, psychological well-being, housing status, medical treatment and health, within either structural or individual discrimination (Link & Phelan, 2001).

The lack of financial resources stigmatised people often experience, can lead to structural discrimination, as when the person cannot afford to live in a secure suburb and as a result becomes a target for assault and less effective services, as good practitioners would rather work in the affluent areas (Link & Phelan, 2001).

A person's individual life chances can be influenced negatively by status loss. For example, the lower status of a person might make the person less attractive to socialise with, or to involve in community activities, or to select as a partner in a business activity that requires social standing (Link & Phelan, 2001).
Once a person is affected by these processes, the cultural stereotype usually affects this person in important ways. The person might form a lay theory about most people rejecting her/him because of the stigma, and this perception can

have serious negative consequences, for example, loss of confidence, defensiveness, or avoidance of potentially threatening situations. The result may be strained and uncomfortable interactions with potential stigmatisers: a shrinking social network, loss of self-esteem, depression, unemployment, income loss and a general loss of quality of life (Link & Phelan, 2001).

Stigma is channelled through social, economic and political power. Power differences in society are taken for granted, so the fact that some people have a mental illness or are wheelchair-bound leads people to focus on the stereotypes associated with the condition rather than on the power difference between people with a disability and people who have no disability.
Once people of a certain type have been stereotyped as undesirable by a more powerful group, as for example the "Blacks" by the "Rednecks", the "undesirable" group then is open to exploitation and even to genocide (Link & Phelan, 2001).

Certainly, the less powerful group can also use stigma related processes about the more powerful group, as patients with a mental illness could label some clinicians as "pill pushers" and stereotype these clinicians as arrogant and cold, and make jokes about them. Yet, although these processes work just like these between "Rednecks" and "Blacks", clinicians would not end up in a stigmatised group simply because patients in a mental hospital do not possess the social, cultural, economic and political power to oppress staff with the dire consequences of discrimination (Link & Phelan, 2001).

There are some exceptions to the general path of stigma. Stigmatised people are not always passive or helpless. In most cases, stigma is internalised by people and can reduce the will to persist in daily life, yet some people are able to challenge stigma and use available resources to resist the discrimination of the more powerful groups. Power differences will certainly restrain these people as well, so they might not fully overcome stigma, yet such people are far from

helpless and passive and may rise above the hopeless seeming situation (Link & Phelan, 2001).
Examples might be the drug user who goes out to speak to the community about his/her experiences and creates discussion in the community, which might lead to better services for users, such as injecting rooms; or the homosexual person, who "comes out of the closet" to fight against discrimination and gay bashings.

Link & Phelan (2001) propose that stigma exists as a matter of degree, because a label can connect a person to many stereotypes, to only a few, or to no stereotypes at all.
The connection between labels and undesirable attributes can be strong or weak. Separation into "in and out groups" can be more or less complete, and the extent of status loss and discrimination can be different. It follows, that some groups are more stigmatised than others (Link & Phelan, 2001).
Herskovits and Mitteness (1994) also recognise a gradient of stigma, depending on the severity of transgressions and sickness in old age (Herskovits & Mitteness, 1994).

Stigma in Dementia

Herskovits and Mitteness (1994) propose in their study of stigma directed against people with dementia, people with incontinence and people with arthritis, that multiple transgressions of key cultural values result in increased stigma. These values include: mastery, productivity, individual responsibility and cleanliness (Herskovits & Mitteness, 1994). It seems that the transgressions involved in dementia in particular, involve an overwhelming assault on adult status, as the person will eventually transgress against all the cultural values stated above, with no hope for improvement. Thus dementia, a mental condition with no known cure or marked improvement so far, is graded as very severe by cultural standards, as people with dementia cannot even hope to come near to successful ageing values (Herskovits & Mitteness, 1994).

Goffman's (1968) perception that the stigmatised person seems to be perceived as less than human is also described by Nolan and associates. Participants in their Irish study referred to the potential for pwd to be treated inhumanely in society. They perceived a diminished value of pwd, negative and demeaning interactions from people in society and from service providers. Enforced isolation seems common for pwd and their carers, due to withdrawal of friends and sometimes even family, and barriers to social participation were described, resulting in social exclusion. Both pwd and his/her carer undergo a significant re-definition of life-space: Many plans have to be abandoned, and alternate arrangements made. Dramatic role changes are also difficult to deal with. Some pwd who have previously been bread winners now are needing support from those they have supported in the past. The loss of these roles often elicits frustration and requires much sensitivity and tact from carers, who not only shoulder extra responsibilities, but also have to console the person who has lost the ability to deal with these responsibilities (Nolan, 2006).

Social isolation of pwd and their carers

Social isolation is a result of the separation and exclusion components of stigma, and it impacts very negatively on pwd and their carers, who are also affected by association with the pwd (Brodaty, 1996).
Nolan and associates describe in their study, that the negative public images, stereotypes and terms associated with dementia are often resulting in 'normals' avoiding to engage with those who have dementia, and the carers keep the behaviours of their pwd 'a dark secret still' (Nolan, 2006, p10).

According to Nolan and associates (2006), the reality of dementia is that many carers of pwd keep their pwd and their problems behind closed doors – isolating themselves from the unkind public. Emotions regarding stigma included anger and hurt due to diminished social networks and negative social encounters, embarrassment and shame if others witnessed inappropriate behaviours in public, and guilt if the carer could not live up to societal expectations of continuation of care at home indefinitely. Dementia was seen as either unifying or dividing families, the latter occurring where family members were unable to accept diagnosis due to stigma related concerns (Nolan, 2006).

Friendship between humans is based on reciprocality, a comparability of thoughts and actions, mostly expressed in language, as exchanges of ideas and feelings in conversations. The further the pwd moves down the path of dementia, the more she or he will lose the ability to use language appropriately, as the capacity to understand abstract concepts and the words attached to them diminishes. The loss of reciprocality in the friendship with people with dementia, is usually the first reason why friends don't visit any longer. Pwd gradually cannot remember words and understand concepts anymore. They increasingly cannot respond as they could in the past, in their unique appealing way. It is like the person is not there anymore, although she or he is physically there, and emotionally intact, and often hurt and frustrated.

Interpersonal connections as roles within the family are different, they undergo huge changes and sometimes with great difficulty, especially with partners. Sons and (mostly) daughters often look after a parent who has dementia. These carers often feel that they need to try to keep the pwd at home to the end, whatever may come, and get terribly upset if they feel they are failing. These caring situations often have a role reversal, when the dominant pwd has to give up responsibility to the dominated (usually the wife or an adult child), yet dislikes it intensely and still demands his or her place (often unreasonably so) while the dominated tiptoes around the pwd and works terribly hard to keep their lives together.

The difficulties of friends and family to cope with the behavioural challenges the pwd and the carer are confronted with, is another major issue, which keeps others away. The general lack of motivation pwd experience, may also make it very difficult to remain socially well connected. All these problems feed into the exclusion component of the stigma of dementia, leading to social isolation.

When old friends and sometimes family members walk away, it becomes really important for pwd and their carers to form new relationships, in carer's support groups and social groups, where pwd and carers mingle, without a worry about unusual behaviours or social appropriateness, as all understand what is happening.

Social interactions are very necessary for all people, but especially for pwd and their carers, to provide the necessary stimulation for this group of people, to prevent further deterioration and to prevent carers being exposed to a situation which may pose a threat to the health of their own brain.

Richard Russell (2001) also describes the withdrawal of friends and family in his study of elderly men who care for wives with dementia. The lack of cooperation of family, disrespect of some services, the invisibility of their work and the isolation they endure while juggling many household tasks they were never trained for, are overwhelming, and yet all fourteen of these men managed their care with nurturing commitment, responsibility and devotion. These men also described hospital and nursing home respite care as very inadequate, and committed themselves to care for their wives at home, out of love and 'to pay her back' for past caring (Russell, 2001, p363).

As is apparent from the foregoing discussion, the stigma related to dementia is seen as something within the person, will usually affect the identity of an individual through the attitudes of other people in society and can also transfer to his/her carers or family members (Benbow & Reynolds, 2000; Brodaty, 1996; Nolan et. al., 2006).

In most cases, stigma is internalised by the bearer. Often older adults will discredit their own abilities according to popular ageist beliefs, and many will describe themselves as "useless". This may lead to a failure to accept services and to lesser participation in community life and life chances (Benbow &

Reynolds, 2000; Link & Phelan, 2001). A major implication of stigma is loss of social networks and social opportunities. Stigma of dementia is further compounded by the fact that pwd and their carers are typically aged over 65 years and they are therefore subject to the disadvantages of ageism.

Stigma of Ageism

There are a small number of people who develop dementia as early as in their forties, but most people are over the age of 55 when diagnosed with dementia (Alzheimers Australia, 2005; AIHW, 2006). Since the prevalence of dementia seems to be more apparent in older adults, another form of stigma also applies to this age group: Ageism. Thus, people with dementia can be stigmatised in two ways: through their mental condition and through being older: a "double whammy', as the participants of Nolan and colleagues' study called it (Nolan et al, 2006; Palmore, 2005).

Thus, ageism is an important component of the full picture of what is happening to pwd.

According to Richard Butler (1975),

> *"Ageism, like all prejudices, has been defined as a process of systematic stereotyping and discrimination against people because they are old, just as racism and sexism accomplish this with skin colour and gender. Old people are categorised as senile, rigid in thought and manner, old fashioned in morality and skills.... Ageism allows the younger generations to see older people as different from themselves; thus they subtly cease to identify with their elders as human beings. "* (Butler,1975, p12).

Ageism, like all prejudices, influences the self-view and behaviour of its victims. The elderly tend to adopt negative definitions of themselves and perpetuate the very stereotypes directed against them, thereby reinforcing society's beliefs (Butler, 1975).

Some expressions of discrimination against people who are older can be seen in the many tasteless jokes involving ageist attitudes, loss of physical and mental abilities, loss of attractiveness, and negative humour. Humourous comments about old women seem more prevalent and more negative than humourous comments about old men (Palmore, 2005).

Maggie Saucier (2004) recognises women's issues of ageing as particularly pertinent, as women are acculturated from a very young age to look like the thinnest of models, but realise that this ideal is unattainable. Thus appearance anxiety and body dissatisfaction starts early in life and becomes even more depressing when midlife sets in and women are faced with a decrease in self-worth through devaluation of older women and age discrimination (Saucier, 2004).

Catherine Sarkisian (2006) proposes in her study about ethnic differences for ageing among older adults, that beliefs about ageing can influence health. The over-attribution of medical symptoms to ageing may have tragic consequences, as these beliefs can lead to passive coping mechanisms, lower rates of health services utilisation and greater mortality. Older adults with lower expectations for ageing are more likely to report sedentary lifestyles, increasing their risk of diabetes mellitus among other diseases. This illness is particularly prevalent in the group of Latino Americans, who have lower age expectations than other groups studied, as Latino seniors believe that exercise and physical activity is inappropriate for older people (Sarkisian, 2006).

Age discrimination also impacts on individuals who care for a partner with dementia, and usually are in the same age group as the pwd. This can have dire effects on income, as not only will the carer experience difficulties in everyday life due to the intense nature of caring for a pwd, but will also be disadvantaged in the labour market due to our society's preoccupation with youth. Although the law provides constraint to discrimination against ageing workers, there is still considerable scope for many forms of discrimination, such as exclusion from promotion or through involuntary retirement, or by denying flexibility in work hours to enable the carer to attend appointments with the pwd (Roscigno et al, 2007)

Use It or Lose It – Risk Factors for Dementia

From the previous discussion of stigma and ageism in dementia, two problems emerge: It seems that pwd not only are exposed to the double effects of stigma in dementia and ageism, but also to the destructive effects of social isolation: lack of stimulation through exclusion, and depression resulting from devaluation and loneliness, which may lead to faster deterioration in their disease path. Another question comes to mind here, could carers of pwd, affected by the social isolation and associated depression while caring for a stigmatised person, be also at a higher risk of developing Alzheimer's Disease (AD)?

Part of the problem in Alzheimer's Disease is neuronal loss, especially in the frontal and temporal lobes (Kimble, 1992). Many of the behaviours of people with Alzheimer's, especially disorientation and subsequent wandering, point to hippocampal damage and/or decrease. Wandering and disorientation in AD seem to be related to general confusion and to deteriorating place learning and memory functions of the hippocampus (Kimble, 1992). Many people with AD cannot adjust to their new environment after a move to a new home, and are very unsettled by this change. Sutherland and Rudy (1989) found, that rats with hippocampal lesions could not orientate to a hidden platform by using other environmental cues. The damage to the hippocampus in AD seems to have a similar effect (Sutherland & Rudy,1989).

Another interesting point to consider is the apparent link between hippocampal shrinkage and depression. From his meta-analysis of the data on history of depression as a risk factor for dementia, Jorm (2001) concluded that depression may be a risk factor for dementia and this possible connection warrants further investigation. Although the present study does not focus on this issue per se, social isolation, a risk factor for depression, is investigated here.

Both depression and dementia seem to make people unmotivated and listless – and the lack of the stimulation of a social network could also impact on this dilemma of inactivity, possibly setting the stage for further deterioration.
There seems to be some evidence for this notion, as the researchers Fratiglioni, Wang, Ericsson, Maytan and Winblad, (2000) found that an extensive social network may delay the onset of dementia by providing emotional and intellectual stimulation and practical support. Poor or limited social networks could increase the risk of dementia by an impressive 60%; poor social support can impact on the immune system and the inflammatory properties of dementia (Fratiglioni et.al., 2000).
Plattner and Erhardt (2000) agree with Fratiglioni and associates (2000), and add that psychosocial problems and lack of stimulation results in neural changes. According to Plattner and Erhardt (2000), research has shown that neither the genetic expression nor the morphological structures of the brain are static, thus our brain can change according to neural activity. The long latency period of time, the 20-30 years when the person is still cognitively functioning, which can elapse between insufficient neural activity, and a diagnosis of AD, could be an indication that all may not be lost. There may be a potential for neuron repair in this period of time by stabilisation of existing synapses and the establishment of new contacts between neurons.
Plattner and Erhardt (2000) further elaborate:

"It has been shown, that the behavioural substrate of synaptic plasticity is activity of the organism, physical, emotional or intellectual" (p434).

Vigorous daily activities stimulate the plasticity of the frontal lobe, and increase the learning potential of the brain (Plattner & Erhardt, 2000). Since most stimulating and satisfying activities are part of a social network, (Plattner &

Erhardt, 2000), the shrinkage of such a network would also mean a reduction in learning potential and a reduction of the plasticity of the frontal lobe. One possible source of stimulation is psychotherapy for people with AD, as psychotherapy is a learning procedure, and usually a satisfying social contact. Behaviour therapy increases pleasant daily activities to overcome depression – why not dementia? (Plattner & Erhardt, 2000)

Other researchers are also working on the same issue. Wilson and associates (2007) explored feelings of loneliness and its relations to Alzheimers Disease in 823 older adults over a four-year period. Participants answered questionnaires to assess loneliness, were evaluated with classifications of dementia and Alzheimers Disease, and were tested regarding their thinking, learning and memory abilities over a five year period.
During the study period, 76 individuals developed dementia that met the criteria for AD. Risk for developing AD increased by approximately 51 percent for each point on the loneliness score, so that a person with a high loneliness score had about 2.1 times greater risk of developing AD than a person with a low score. The findings did not change significantly when researchers factored in markers of social isolation, such as a small network of family and friends and infrequent social activities (Wilson et. al., 2007).
The fact that loneliness during life was related to the brain changes signifying a post mortem diagnosis of AD indicates that loneliness contributes to risk of AD, like old age contributes to the risk of dementia (Wilson et. al., 2007).

Wilson states that humans need healthy social interactions with other humans to remain physically and psychologically healthy and to achieve a good quality of life. The results of the study conducted by Wilson and colleagues suggest that people who are lonely and subsequently depressed may be more vulnerable to dementia. Behaviour change (i.e. through behavioural therapy), physical and mental exercises, an increased social network and some medications (Wilson et al, 2007), such as cholinesterase inhibitors, could help decrease the risk of dementia in older adults and at the same time, prevent further deterioration for some time (Truscott, 2003).

Underlying psychological or medical conditions, which could cause dementia, such as depression, vascular problems, vitamin deficiencies or hypothyroidism, need to be corrected. And planning is paramount, writes Phyllis Dyck, who is a person with dementia. She found innovative ways of caring for herself, physically, mentally, emotionally and spiritually. She took responsibility for her wellness today, while she was planning for future wellness, further down the track of disability, informing her family about her plans, to work together to make this experience as pleasant as possible (Dyck, 2006).

Recently, Michael Valenzuela (2006) provided the most convincing evidence yet that complex mental activity across people's lives significantly reduces their risk for dementia. Valenzuela did a meta-analysis across 22 studies, with data from 29,000 people from around the world, and all the studies agreed that mentally stimulating activities, even late in life, have a protective effect against dementia. In a separate study, conducted over three years Valenzuela (2003) found that brief mental activation training increased the volume of structures in the medial temporal lobe. Social activity was mentioned as one of the most valuable past times, as nothing apparently stimulates as much as an intelligent partner in conversation and interactions (Valenzuela, 2003).

This information really points to the use it or lose it principle, and to the value of social interactions in life, to keep our brain healthy and free from dementia and depression.

Apparently, a lack of social, recreational and industrial activity over 20-30 years, slowly prepares our brain for the deterioration of AD and other dementias, and the boredom encountered in many institutions of aged care is a very negative condition, as it can make people both physically and psychologically ill, further adding to the problems for which residential care was required.

The literature increasingly authenticates the importance of social support, for both the pwd and his or her carer in the community. It is not only necessary to prevent pwd from deteriorating at a faster rate, it also seems important to protect carers of pwd from the lack of stimulation which is experienced in social isolation, to prevent at least some of the predicted increase in dementia which communities may experience in the future.

Change in Social Support

Many of the changes in older age groups have to do with losses: loss of abilities, loss of independence, loss of income and financial freedom, and also loss of peers in the age cohort through loss of mobility and death.
Krause (1999) investigated the change in social support during later life, using 14 measures of social support. The large number of diverse measures used to assess social support reflects the idea that social support is a complex phenomenon with many dimensions that is not captured by a unitary measure of support (Barrera, 1986). Thus, for instance, it is not sufficient to assess the frequency of contact with friends/family as an index of social support (Barrera, 1986).

Krause not only used an aggregate approach to measure change, he also investigated change on an individual level, to capture opposite movements of change, i.e. improvement in social support, within this cohort (Krause, 1999). In terms of aggregate change, Krause noted that there is an overall loss of social support, however for some individuals there was an increase in social support.

He found that substantial change took place during the relatively short period of four years in the lives of people over 65 years of age, and that the change is not uniform or systematic across the entire study sample. People of this age are a very heterogenous group, depending on genes, lifestyles and life chances

throughout their lives, and accordingly there appears to be considerable individual level change taking place (Krause, 1999).
Krause also found that change is more likely to be observed with some social support measures than with others; for example, measures of perceived social support are more stable than other dimensions of social support; tangible support is not provided as often as emotional and informational support by older people at the aggregate level; and some older people have more contact with their families over time, but some have less, depending on individual circumstances(Krause, 1999).

Nolan et al. stated that there is a need for the investigation of social isolation as part of the stigma process in dementia. It seems that social isolation of pwd and carers has not been researched sufficiently so far (Nolan et al, 2006), despite the potential for very serious negative effects of social isolation on both pwd and their carers. Nolan et al. stated that:

"research that investigates the nature of relationships between those with dementia and those surrounding them, family, neighbours, the local community, may help illuminate how stigma and its components affect social interaction and constructs such as social distance" (pp. 14-15)

The Present Study
Aims and Rationale

The present study aimed to investigate change of social support for people with dementia (pwd) and their carers at two points in time: before diagnosis and after diagnosis. No study was located which has assessed changes in social support of pwd and their carers.
In an older population, a reduction of friends is not unusual, simply because more people pass away in this cohort thus reducing social circles. It is expected, that pwd and carers are losing social support at a greater rate than healthy people in

society, and therefore are experiencing social isolation more often than the general population of older adults.

Current research seems to have documented that social isolation could be a factor in faster deterioration of pwd. Yet the carers, being trapped in the same isolation as the pwd, could also be at risk. Through lack of social stimulation, carers could be entering the latency period of 20-30 years, which precedes the diagnosis of dementia and during which people slowly develop the illness while they are still cognitively functioning (Fratiglioni et al, 2000; Jorm, 2001; Kimble, 1992; Plattner & Erhardt, 2000, Valenzuela, 2006; Wilson et al., 2007).

Many older adults seem to lose peers through natural causes, reducing their social network, leading to fewer contacts and less social stimulation.

One rationale for this and other related research is to provide the basis for a case for the government to sponsor more programs, not only to educate carers and the public and to form carer's support groups, but also to provide social programs that bring pwd and carers together in a non-threatening environment, and allow them to have rewarding and stimulating social experiences, to keep them as healthy as possible and make it worthwhile living again.

In the current study, frequency of social interactions and received support may be seen as equally important. Contact with friends and kin and different kinds of help received involve social contact with others, conversations and face to face interactions. Social contact stimulates the mind and, according to an increasing number of researchers, multiple factors such as loneliness, depression and lack of stimulation through lack of social contact seem to facilitate the premature onset of dementia (Kimble, 1992; Fratiglioni et al, 2000; Plattner & Erhardt, 2000; Jorm, 2001; Valenzuela, 2006; Wilson and associates, 2007).

At the time of the current study, there was no research found that addressed the issue of changes in social support in a healthy older population in Australia. Since the US population of healthy older adults, still living in the community, seemed to be culturally quite similar to the Australian older population, the study used Krause's US older population to compare the differences in the magnitude of change between these two populations.

Hypotheses

It was predicted that there will be a greater of loss of social support for the sample of carers of pwd in Australia , than for the sample of healthy older adults in the US used in Krause's (1999) study. However, the change in social support measures were not predicted to be uniform across measures.

A number of additional analyses were undertaken in the present study. Firstly, the difference in the change in social support associated with different kinds of dementia (Alzheimers, Cardiovascular and Other dementias) was compared. It was hypothesised that carers of pwd with Other dementia would experience the greatest change in social support, because in these types of dementia personality changes often take place and pwd become less sociable.

Secondly, the difference between early, mid and late stage dementia were explored with respect to changes in social support. It was predicted that deterioration of social relations is most likely to occur in the mid and late stage of dementia, when forgetfulness and frustration with lost abilities are causing unusual behaviours. In the early stage, where deterioration of pwd is not quite as apparent, it is not expected that social support will have changed from before diagnosis.

The final analysis assessed the differences in social support for groups between those carers of pwd who had made new friends and those who had not made new friends to replace lost friends. It was expected that pwd and their carers with new friends would experience more support than pwd and carers that were not able to make new friends.

Method

Participants

Participants were recruited through Alzheimer's Australia NSW. Due to the vulnerability of pwd, and also potential inability of pwd to provide required information, carers of pwd were interviewed.
Carers were selected in a simple random sampling procedure from the data base of family carers at Alzheimer's Australia NSW.
The recruitment procedure involved sending a letter to carers of pwd, inviting them to participate in this study on social support.
Carers were from an Australian background, living in the Sydney Metropolitan area, Newcastle, Wollongong and in NSW. Some carers were still living with their pwd, some pwd were in residential care, and other pwd had passed away and the carer was responding in retrospect.
Respondents were family members of pwd, either spouses or sons or daughters of pwd. From the 500 carers of pwd, who were approached to participate, 174 (35%) responded within the timeframe given to return the questionnaire.
Carers were not asked to supply their ages. However, since dementia usually occurs over 65 years of age, and carers are typically of a similar age to pwd, the present sample of pwd and their carers are assumed to be part of the older population of Australia.
The project was approved by the School of Humanities and Social Sciences Ethics Committee, Charles Sturt University (Appendix A).
Participants received the survey in the mail. In total 500 survey packages were mailed out and 174 were returned (35%).

Thirty-one of the surveys could not be used, because they were either not filled in at all, with a short note stating why the recipient thought it inappropriate to respond, and some were only partially filled in, with large parts missing. A total of 143 questionnaires were used in the study, 28.6% response rate in total.

Measures

The current study employed a self-report questionnaire developed by Neal Krause (1999) to assess change in social support in later life. Krause (1999) conducted a longitudinal study, probing the change in social support over a period of four years (Krause, 1999).

Krause (1999) measured participants at two points to evaluate changes in social support over a four year period. Thus the social support of healthy adults aged 65 years and over was initially measured (wave 1) and then measured again four years later (wave 2). The scale he developed contains many items relevant to social support, exploring many dimensions of social support: not only frequency of social interactions, but also emotional, informational and tangible support received and provided, satisfaction with support, anticipated support and negative encounters with others.

Krause (1999) not only used an aggregate approach to measure changes in social support in older age groups, he also investigated change on an individual level to capture opposite movement in change. Krause (1999) measured a random sample of between 535 and 605 older adults in North America, who still lived in the community. The difference in numbers of participants resulted from sample attrition and death of some of the participants (Krause, 1999).

This method of measuring change in social support was recognised as particularly appropriate for this study, and Professor Krause gave his approval to use his scale and to adapt it as required for the current research.

To address changes in social support in different groups of people with dementia, both in terms of the type of diagnosis, for instance Alzheimer's and Cardiovascular dementia as well the stage of dementia (early, mid, late) the following preliminary questions were added to Krause's questionnaire:
How long since your pwd has been diagnosed?
What stage of dementia is your pwd in? (early, mid or late stage)
What type of dementia has your pwd been diagnosed with?
(Alzheimers, cardiovascular, or other)
After diagnosis, have you been able to make new friends in a carer's group or other social activity?
If yes, was this social activity provided by a government organisation?
If no, please circle one option:
no program or group available; no time to go out; other;
The part of the question "other" elicited comments from carers, very appropriate and valid to the study, from 85 of the 143 respondents. Some of these comments were used in the discussion.

Participants were asked for information regarding approximately how much time had lapsed between diagnosis of dementia and the current interview. This would give a time frame regarding how long it took for social support to change.

The question regarding the type of dementia aimed to explore differences in the impact of types of dementia on social isolation, and the question pertaining to ability to make new friends probed the possibility that old friends have been replaced by new ones, which could be hiding the fact that old friends have dropped off after diagnosis. The question regarding the type of social activity was included to elicit information about where pwd and carers can actually go to make friends, and if this event was provided privately or by government, and the basic reasons pwd and carers may not be able to participate in an activity.

This information was used to establish changes in social support for the groups of carers as a whole, as well as to explore whether sub-groups of carers had different experiences of changes in social support.

The modified questionnaire used in the present study is presented in Appendix D.
The questionnaire by Krause (1999) uses three informal social support measures, social embeddedness, support received or provided and perceived support.
Reliability estimates from Krause's study for each scale are as follows.

Social Embeddedness

The first scale of social embeddedness or frequency of contact with others, is expressed by the measures contact with friends and contact with kin (Krause, 1999) which each contain three items.
A high score on these items denotes higher contact frequency with friends and family. The internal consistency reliability estimate (Cronbach's Alpha) for the scale items assessing contact with friends was .649 at wave1, and .666 at wave2; for the items assessing contact with kin, Cronbach's Alpha at wave1 was .595, and .612 at wave2.

Received and provided support

The second measure of social support, received support or provided support consists of three groups of measures.
The amount of tangible help actually received from others or provided to others, emotional support received from others or provided to others and informational support received from others or provided to others (Krause, 1999).
Again, these forms of social contact, especially emotional and informational support received and provided, presume face to face, telephone contact or

correspondence – all forms of stimulating conversation, whether they involve support received or support provided.

A high score on these items means that carers of pwd received or provided assistance on these items more often.

Cronbach's Alpha for these items was as follows: Emotional support received at wave1 was .823, at wave2. was 807; emotional support provided at wave1 was .833 and at wave2 was .850. Tangible help received at wave1 was .696, at wave2 was .745; tangible help provided at wave1 was .634, at wave2 it was .697. Informational support received at wave1 was .758, at wave was 2 .804; informational support provided at wave1 was .846, at wave it was 2 .838.

Perceived Satisfaction with Support

The third measure of social support, perceived satisfaction with support or subjective evaluations of supportive exchanges, is measured by satisfaction with support, negative interaction and anticipated support.

Satisfaction with support received involves three indicators which relate to separate question groups of social support, satisfaction with emotional, tangible and informational support received from others. These forms of perceived support impact on perceived quality of life, which in turn impacts on the well-being of individuals. A separate binary score is used for each of these items, where a value of one indicates satisfaction and a value of zero indicates dissatisfaction (Krause, 1999).

Satisfaction with support provided contained only one question for all kinds of satisfaction with support given to other people (Krause, 1999).

Negative interaction was assessed using 4 items. This measure is included to acknowledge the fact that not all social support is positive in nature and indeed negative interactions can offset or outweigh the benefits of reciprocal support (Krause, 1999). A high score on these items indicates more negative interactions for respondents. The internal consistency reliability estimate for these items at wave1 was .830 and at wave2 .799.

The final measure of perceived satisfaction with support is anticipated support. Anticipated support measures the belief that others will provide support in the future should this become necessary. Anticipated support seems to exert especially valuable benefits in later life. The belief that friends and family will provide assistance in the future, should the need arise, seems reassuring to older adults. A high score on this set of questions reflects greater anticipated support (Krause, 1999). Cronbach's Alpha for these questions at wave1 was .819 and at wave2 it was .868.

Carers in this study were interviewed only once, yet the study required two conditions to assess change in social support. For this reason, the inclusion of a 'before diagnosis' and 'after diagnosis' section was required with each question, to create a similar situation to Neal Krause's "first wave" and "second wave" conditions. Thus the present study explored the status of social interactions before diagnosis of dementia (past) and after diagnosis (now).

Procedure

Participants received the surveys in the mail. Each survey package contained the modified social support scale and an information statement. The information statement included information about any terminology, which might be unclear, for example the meaning of early stage, mid stage or late stage dementia, which was important to the understanding of the preliminary questions.

A copy of the information statement is contained in Appendix B.

Data Analysis

Data analysis was completed using the Statistical Package for Social Sciences (SPSS).
Internal consistency analyses were performed on all measures of social support. Paired sample t-tests were performed to compare social support (on all measures) before and after diagnosis.
Although performing multiple t-tests raises the experimentwise error rate, t-tests were selected as these analyses enable one to assess the specific predictions of the present study. Thus for instance, although using an ANOVA lowers the experimentwise error rate, it would not have been possible to test the hypotheses of this study using ANOVA.

The first groups to be compared included a group of healthy older adults in America, and a group of carers of pwd in Australia.
Further subgroups of participants were compared to determine whether there were any differences in the changes of social support for the different groups. As such, the differences in change in social support measures for carers of pwd with Alzheimers, Cardiovascular and Other types of dementia were assessed.
Differences in change in social support were also compared for carers of pwd in the Early, Mid and Late stages of dementia. The last comparison of changes was performed with a group of carers of pwd who were able to make new friends (Newfriends) after diagnosis of their person and carers of pwd who were not able to make new friends (Nofriends).

Results

(Tables in Appendix C)

Neal Krause (1999) conducted a longitudinal study assessing change in social support during later life. Participants were measured twice, with a four year gap in between measures (referred to as Wave 1 and Wave 2). No Australian study was found, which explored the changes of social support in a general population of older adults, so Neal Krause's (1999) study seemed appropriate to use as a baseline comparison for the Australian sample of carers of pwd. The present study was cross-sectional and carers were asked to indicate their level of social support before and after the diagnosis of dementia.

Krause (1999) used a random sample of between 535 and 605 older adults in North America. Due to a number of factors including attrition and death, the sample size decreased over the four year period.

The current study endeavoured to evaluate differences in changes of social support between two culturally similar populations in Western society, a general older population in the US and a population of carers of pwd in Australia. Neal Krause's (1999) study involved a predominantly healthy older population over 65 years of age and still living in the community, and it seems of great interest to note the differences in the change of social support between this population and a population of older adults with dementia and their carers.

In the present study, the sample of carers of pwd was asked to answer the same set of questions twice, one relating to the social support experienced before diagnosis (BD, past), the other relating to the social support experienced after diagnosis (AD, present). This arrangement likened the questionnaire to Neal Krause's (1999) longitudinal study, which was conducted in 1992/93 (first wave or W1) and in 1996/97 (second wave or W2). The present study included data from 143 participants in NSW.

The results of the analyses that assessed the change in social support, as measured by the mean for each measure of social support, for the sample of carers of people with dementia, are presented in Table1. For purposes of comparison, the corresponding data from Neal Krause's (1999) study is also contained in Table1. This table also presents the standard deviations and the correlations between before and after conditions of the survey scores.

Correlations were included as t-tests and could only indicate aggregate change (mean change). Where there is a difference between the results of the t-tests and the correlations, this suggests that individual level change is different from aggregate change (see Krause, 1999). For instance, in cases where the t statistic is significant but the correlation is low, this suggests that the sample is not homogenous but rather that the social support of some participants increases after diagnosis while for others there is a decrease in social support.
The results are presented as 14 separate t-tests for both the current study and that of Neal Krause (1999). Significant differences in the mean levels of social support were detected in half of the tests, similar to Krause's results. The direction of change, however, was not always in the same direction in the two studies.

Further, in light of the fact that the present study investigated the social support of carers of pwd as opposed to a random elderly sample, there were a number of additional analyses undertaken in this study.

The preliminary questions, which were added to Neal Krause's (1999) questionnaire, classified respondents into various groups of types of dementia, stages of dementia and also types of social opportunities regarding making new friends to replace the friends they may have lost. By eliciting this information, comparisons could be made between groups of pwd and their carers, to gain insight into possible differences between such groups.

Three groups emerged from this questioning, Alzheimers, Cardiovascular and Other (included dementia other than Alzheimers and Cardiovascular, for instance Lewy Body Dementia). Thus, the mean difference of the Alzheimers group was compared to those of the Cardiovascular group and the Other (types of dementia) group. Further, the mean difference of the Early, Mid and Late stage groups were compared, as were those of the New Friends Made and the No Friends Made group.

Reliability Analyses for each Measure of Social Support

The questionnaire by Krause (1999) uses three informal social support measures, social embeddedness, support received or provided and perceived support.
Reliability estimates were computed for these measures for the current study, and the values are reported as follows.

Social Embeddedness

The first scale of social embeddedness or frequency of contact with others, is expressed by these measures: Contact with friends and contact with kin (Krause, 1999) which each contain three items.
A high score on these items denotes higher contact frequency with friends and family.
The internal consistency reliability estimate (Cronbach's Alpha) for the scale items assessing contact with friends was .787 before diagnosis, and .662 after diagnosis; for the items assessing contact with kin, Cronbach's Alpha before diagnosis was .725, and .580 after diagnosis.

Received and provided support

The second measure of social support, received support or provided support consists of three groups of measures.
The amount of tangible help actually received from others or provided to others, emotional support received from others or provided to others and informational support received from others or provided to others (Krause, 1999).

Again, these forms of social contact, especially emotional and informational support received and provided, presume face to face, telephone contact or correspondence – all forms of stimulating conversation, whether they involve support received or support provided.

A high score on these items means that carers and pwd received or provided assistance on these items more often.

Cronbach's Alpha for these items was as follows: Emotional support received before diagnosis was .865, after diagnosis .873; emotional support provided before diagnosis was .851 and after diagnosis .859. Tangible help received before diagnosis was .825, after diagnosis .814; tangible help provided before diagnosis was .793, after diagnosis it was .794. Informational support received before diagnosis was .842, after diagnosis .831; informational support provided after diagnosis was .870, after diagnosis .873.

Perceived Satisfaction with Support

The third measure of social support, perceived satisfaction with support or subjective evaluations of supportive exchanges, is measured by satisfaction with support, negative interaction and anticipated support.

Satisfaction with support received involves three indicators which relate to separate question groups of social support, satisfaction with emotional support received, tangible support received and informational support received from others. These forms of perceived support impact on perceived quality of life, which in turn impacts on the well-being of individuals. A separate binary score is used for each of these items, where a value of one indicates satisfaction and a value of zero indicates dissatisfaction (Krause, 1999).

Satisfaction with support provided contained only one question for all kinds of satisfaction with support given to other people in their social network (Krause, 1999).

Negative interaction was assessed using 4 items. This measure is included to acknowledge the fact that not all social support is positive in nature and indeed negative interactions can offset or outweigh the benefits of reciprocal support (Krause, 1999). A high score on these items indicates more negative interactions for respondents. The internal consistency reliability estimate for these items before diagnosis is .868, after diagnosis .845.

The final measure of perceived satisfaction with support is anticipated support. Anticipated support measures the belief that others will provide support in the future should this become necessary. Anticipated support seems to exert especially valuable benefits in later life. The belief that friends and family will provide assistance in the future, should the need arise, seems reassuring to older adults. A high score on this set of questions reflects greater anticipated support (Krause, 1999). Cronbach's Alpha for these questions before diagnosis was .903, after diagnosis .854. Reliability estimates for all measures were sufficiently high (>.7), thus suggesting that Krause's questionnaire was reliable for the sample used in the present study.

Significant changes in social support for the Australian carers of pwd.

Contact with friends (BD$\bar{X}$=7.706, AD$\bar{X}$=6.091, $t(142)$=-10.019, $p<0.01$) and contact with kin (BD$\bar{X}$=7.203, AD$\bar{X}$=6.357, $t(142)$=-6.476, $p<0.01$) revealed the greatest loss in social support. This was closely followed in order by tangible help provided (BD$\bar{X}$=6.259, AD$\bar{X}$=5.525, $t(142)$=-4.049, $p<0.01$), satisfaction with tangible help received (BD$\bar{X}$=0.780, AD$\bar{X}$=0.590, $t(142)$=4.033, $p<0.01$), and satisfaction with emotional support received (BD$\bar{X}$=0.790, AD$\bar{X}$=0.650, $t(142)$=-3.459, $p<0.05$).
Tangible help received seemed to rise significanlty (BD$\bar{X}$=5.308, AD$\bar{X}$=5.713, $t(142)$=2.411, $p<0.01$) and information received rose markedly for pwd and carers (BD$\bar{X}$=5.364, AD$\bar{X}$=6.629, $t(142)$=7.516, $p<0.01$)

In the present study, not all of the other measures assessing social support showed significant change. However, it is of note that a loss was expressed in emotional support provided, satisfaction with information received, satisfaction with support provided and negative interactions. An insignificant gain was expressed in emotional support received, information provided and anticipated support.

Comparing Australian and US samples

Contact with friends was higher in the Australian sample of carers of pwd before diagnosis (BD$\bar{X}$=7.706) than in the US sample wave1 (W1$\bar{X}$=7.356), and contact with friends was lower in the Australian sample after diagnosis (AD$\bar{X}$=6.091) than in the US sample wave2 (W2$\bar{X}$=6.931), indicating a much greater loss of friends in the Australian sample of carers of pwd compared with a sample of healthy older Americans.

Contact with kin also showed the trend of greater losses of social support for carers of pwd in the Australian sample (BD $\bar{X}$=7.203, AD$\bar{X}$=6.357), than for the US sample (W1 $\bar{X}$=7.557, W2 $\bar{X}$=7.355).

Although the loss of kin seems to occur only about half as often as the loss of friends for both samples, the Australian sample of carers of pwd had lost four times as much contact with friends and family (1.615 points and 0.846 points) than the US sample (0.425 points vs. 0.202 points, respectively).

The values for each item of the scales measuring contact with friends and kin indicate, that carers and pwd seem to have all but given up on venturing out, to visit family or friends. Family seems to visit and stay in contact by telephone, although significantly less often than before diagnosis. Friends do not come to visit anymore, and hardly stay in touch by telephone or mail.

Emotional support received did not change significantly for either sample, indicating stability of the measure. The sample of carers of pwd gained from

$BD\bar{X}=9.371$ to $AD\bar{X}=9.699$; the US sample from $W1\bar{X}=10.409$ to $W2\bar{X}=10.825$, a slightly greater gain for the US sample.

Tangible help received also showed the same trend. The mean for the Australian sample increased from $BD\bar{X}=5.308$ to $AD\bar{X}=5.713$; the US sample from $W1\bar{X}=5.478$ to $W2\bar{X}=5.85$, a slightly greater gain for the Australian sample. Informational support received presented an upwards trend for both samples. The Australian sample gained from $BD\bar{X}=5.364$ to $AD\bar{X}=6.629$, around five times the gain in points of the US sample with $W1\bar{X}=4.977$ to $\bar{X}=5.228$.

Emotional support provided showed a non significant downwards trend for both samples. The Australian sample lost from $BD\bar{X}=10.28$ to $AD\bar{X}=9.895$ and the US sample lost from $W1\bar{X}=10.553$ to $W2\bar{X}=10.324$; this amounts to a greater loss for the Australian sample.

Tangible support provided displayed a very similar non significant downwards trend in the Australian and US samples. The Australian sample lost from $BD\bar{X}=6.259$ to $AD\bar{X}=5.525$, and the US sample lost from $W1\bar{X}=5.928$ to $W2\bar{X}=5.195$. This again represents a loss in tangible support provided to others. For Informational support provided, the data went in opposite directions for the two samples: The Australian sample ($BD\bar{X}=5.860$ to $AD\bar{X}=6.063$) gained around the same amount as the US sample ($W1\bar{X}=5.599$ to $W2\bar{X}=5.383$) lost in support, however, neither change was significant.

There was a significant decrease in satisfaction with emotional support in the present study ($BD\bar{X}=0.790$ to $AD\bar{X}=0.650$), whereas the US sample only dropped insignificantly from $W1\bar{X}=0.890$ to $W2\bar{X}=0.860$.

Satisfaction with tangible support received showed similar results. There was a significant decrease in tangible support for carers of pwd ($BD\bar{X}=0.780$ to $AD\bar{X}=0.590$), while the US sample only dropped insignificantly from $W1\bar{X}=0.916$ to $W2\bar{X}=0.892$.

Satisfaction with informational support received showed an insignificant loss for the Australian sample (BD$\bar{X}$=0.740 to AD$\bar{X}$=0.670), and an insignificant gain for the US sample (W1$\bar{X}$=0.880 to W2$\bar{X}$=0.889), which amounts to a change in opposite directions.

Satisfaction with support provided showed an insignificant loss for the Australian sample of BD$\bar{X}$=0.760 to BD$\bar{X}$0.710, while the US sample rose in satisfaction from W1$\bar{X}$=0.674 to W2$\bar{X}$=0.676.

Negative interactions increased for the Australian sample (BD$\bar{X}$=6.650 to AD$\bar{X}$=6.902) and dropped for the US sample (W1$\bar{X}$=5.898 to W2$\bar{X}$=5.578).

Anticipated support was reasonably stable for both the sample of pwd (BD$\bar{X}$=8.664, to AD$\bar{X}$=8.776), and the US sample (W1$\bar{X}$=10.240 to W2$\bar{X}$=10.178).

The greater homogeneity of the Australian sample of carers of pwd, compared with the US sample of the general older population, was expressed in 9 out of 14 lower standard deviations between paired samples for the Australian study, mostly across the social contact with friends and kin data, and also the received and provided support. In these areas of questioning there seems greater agreement in the sample of carers of pwd than in the US sample.

This pattern changes with the data indicating satisfaction. Only 'satisfaction with support provided' has a lower standard deviation for carers of pwd than the healthy older adults sample. Satisfaction with emotional and tangible support and information received, all have higher standard deviations, together with decreasing means (before and after diagnosis), indicating more differences between participants in the sample of carers of pwd than in the healthy older population.

For carers of pwd, a rising standard deviation for negative interactions also expresses a growing discrepancy in experience, indicating that although the means are expressing a small increase in negative interactions with others overall, some individuals have a decrease. This is unlike the American older adults, who show a decrease in both means and standard deviations for negative interactions, indicating that a greater number of participants seem to experience a decrease in negative events.

The standard deviations for anticipated support were lower in the sample of carers of pwd than in the healthy older sample.

Correlations

Correlations between the wave1 and wave2 or between the before diagnosis and after diagnosis measures, can express discrepancies between data indicating that for some participants there is an increase in social support while for others social support decreases. For example, the satisfaction data for informational support received (BD$\bar{X}$=0.740, AD$\bar{X}$=0.670, t(142)=-1.78, p<0.05), and for support provided (BD$\bar{X}$=0.760, AD$\bar{X}$=0.710, t(142)=-1.096, p<0.05), shows very little change in the means. However, as suggested by Krause (1999), this may be misleading, as the correlations for these items are low (.470 and .466, respectively). Although the means for these items suggest that very little change has taken place between measures, the coefficient of .470 only explains 22% of the variance in the follow up measure, and the coefficient of .466 only explains 21.7%. This indicates that the rank order of study participants must have changed between measures and individual change has taken place. This is not depicted by the aggregate measures.

However, it was not considered essential, to employ the Q^2 statistic used by Neal Krause (1999) to elucidate individual level change, as most of the aggregate data have captured the predicted trend, that the sample of carers of pwd would be losing social support at a much greater rate than the sample of a general older population of a similar society.

It seems that the direction of change in social support of carers of pwd after diagnosis is comparable to that of healthy older adults (Krause, 1999). However, the change in the former group is of a far greater magnitude.

Although pwd and their carers are receiving a slight increase in emotional and tangible support and report a great increase in informational support, family and friends are not staying in touch as they did before diagnosis of dementia, thus decreasing the social stimulation pwd and carers need.

Alzheimers, Cardiovascular dementia and Other dementias

Table 2 depicts the means, standard deviations and correlations related to change of social support in the Alzheimers (Alz), Cardiovascular (Cardio) and Other types of dementia (Other) groups.

The groups of people with Alzheimers, Cardiovascular dementia and Other types of dementia were approximately consistent with the population distribution of these types of dementia. People with Alzheimers made up 72% of the group (n=102), compared with an estimated 65% in the population, people with cardiovascular dementia made up 20% of the group (n=29), compared with 25% in the population, and people with other types of dementia were 8% of the group (n=12), compared with 10% in the population.

In the item 'contact with friends' the means reduce dramatically in all three groups after diagnosis (Alz BD$\bar{X}$=7.578, AD$\bar{X}$=6.039, t(101)=-8.661, p<0.01; Cardio BD$\bar{X}$=8.103, AD$\bar{X}$=6.620, t(28)=-4.043, p<0.01; Other BD$\bar{X}$=7.833, AD$\bar{X}$=5.250=, t(11)= -0.300, p<0.05). Standard deviations all seemed to reduce in the after diagnosis condition, the most significant reduction was noted in the Other group, from 2.406 to 1.055. Correlations were low, Alz .485, Cardio .419 and Other -.090.

In the item 'contact with kin' which reduces a little less than the previous item, only the Alzheimers and Cardio groups have significant reductions in social contact, the group with Other types of dementia, although showing a reduction in contact with kin, seems not to have enough participants to score in the significant range (Alz BD$\bar{X}$=7.216, AD$\bar{X}$=6.324, t(101)=-5.752, p<0.01; Cardio BD$\bar{X}$=7.138, AD$\bar{X}$=6.517, t(28)=-2.306, p<0.05; Other BD$\bar{X}$=7.250, AD$\bar{X}$=6.250, t(11)=-1.864, p<0.05). Standard deviations rose for Alz and Cardio groups, but decreased for the Other group. Correlations are .636, .617 and .522, respectively, for the three groups.

The next item 'informational support received' showed a significant gain for all three groups is (Alz BD$\bar{X}$=5.353, AD$\bar{X}$=6.363, t(102)=5.685, p<0.01; Cardio BD$\bar{X}$=5.552, AD$\bar{X}$=7.756, t(28)=3.727, p<0.05; Other BD$\bar{X}$=5.000, AD$\bar{X}$=7.333, t(11)=3.766, p<0.05). Standard deviations reduced for Alz, and increased for Cardio and Other groups. Correlations were low for Alz (.557), very low for Cardio (.122) and relatively high for the Other group (.690)

Emotional Support provided was only significantly lower for the Alzheimers group (BD$\bar{X}$=10.206, AD$\bar{X}$=9.745, t(102)=-2.068, p<0.05), although participants in the Cardio group also had lower scores in the after diagnosis condition. Interestingly, participants in the Other group had increased scores in the after diagnosis condition, although not significant, indicating that this group is providing more emotional support now than before diagnosis.
Standard deviations rose slightly for the Alz group, fell for the Cardio group and rose sharply for the Other group. Correlations were .657, .626 and .499 for the three groups, indicating some individual change especially for the Other group.

Tangible help provided reduced for all three groups, but only significantly for the Alz and Cardio groups (AlzBD$\bar{X}$=6.196, AD$\bar{X}$=5.529, t(102)=-3.126, p<0.05; CardioBD$\bar{X}$=6.586, AD$\bar{X}$=5.448, t(28)=-2.850, p<0.05).
Standard deviations were stable for Alz, decreased for Cardio and rose steeply for Other, indicating an increase in variability in the Other sample. The correlations for the before and after conditions were relatively large for all groups, .573 for Alz, .567 for Cardio and .701 for Other.

Satisfaction with emotional support provided fell significantly for Alz and Cardio, but was stable for Other (AlzBD$\bar{X}$=0.780, AD$\bar{X}$=0.670, t(102)=-2.408, p<0.05;

CardioBD$\bar{X}$=0.900, AD$\bar{X}$=0.620, t(28)=-3.266, p<0.05). Standard deviations rose for Alz and Cardio groups, but were stable for the Other group. The correlation between before and after diagnosis was low for Alz (.388), moderate for Cardio (.435), but high for Other (.657).

Satisfaction with tangible support received also declined significantly for Alz and Cardion and only very slightly for Other (AlzBD$\bar{X}$=0.760, AD$\bar{X}$=0.630, t(102)=-2.540, p<0.05; CardioBD$\bar{X}$=0.930, AD$\bar{X}$=0.550, t(28)=-4.137, p<0.01). Standard deviations rose slightly for Alz, more strongly for Cardio, and were stable for Other. Correlations were very low for Alz (.290) and Cardio (.302) and moderate for Other (.507).

Satisfaction with information received fell significantly for Cardio only (CardioBD$\bar{X}$=0.860, AD$\bar{X}$=0.690, t(28)=-2.415, p<0.05). Standard deviations rose slightly for Cardio, but remained stable for the Alz group and the Other group. The correlation for Cardio was .596, for Alz .429, and for Other .507.

Negative interactions increased significantly for the Alz group (AlzBD$\bar{X}$=6.657, AD$\bar{X}$=7.098, t(102)=2.081, p<0.05), but not for Cardio. The Other group showed decreased negative interactions, but this change was not significant. Standard deviations remained quite stable for Alz and Cardio, but decreased sharply for Other. Correlations were large for all groups, .701 for Alz, .551 for Cardio and .922 for Other.

All other items in this grouping of samples did not show significant changes in means, standard deviations or unusually low or high correlations.

Early- Mid and Late stages of dementia

Table 3 depicts the means, standard deviations and correlations related to change of social support in the Early stage (Early), Mid stage (Mid) and Late stages (Late) groups.

People with early dementia made up 24% (n=34) of the total sample, people with mid stage dementia made up 59% (n=84), and people with late stage dementia were 17% (n=25) of the sample.

The first item, 'Contact with friends', presented a significant loss for all three stages of dementia. Early stage dementia showed the smallest decrease in means, indicating a moderate loss of friends (BD$\bar{X}$=7.265, AD$\bar{X}$=6.588, t(33)=-3.100, p<0.05), followed by mid stage dementia with a very severe loss of friends (BD$\bar{X}$=7.857, AD$\bar{X}$=5.857, t(83)=-1.554, p<0.01), and late stage dementia with another severe loss of friends (BD$\bar{X}$=7.800, AD$\bar{X}$=6.200, t(24)=-4.328, p<0.01). Standard deviations rose moderately for Early, and decreased for Mid and Late stages, indicating a change to increased homogeneity between participants in the two latter stages. Correlations were relatively high for Early (.775), very low for Mid (.299) and moderate for Late stage (.500).

Contact with kin showed a significant loss of family for Early (BD$\bar{X}$=7.235, AD$\bar{X}$=6.765, t(33)=-2.098, p<0.05) and Mid stages (BD$\bar{X}$=7.190, AD$\bar{X}$=6.155, t(83)=-6.042, p<0.01) of pwd and their carers, and a loss, but not quite significant for Late stage pwd and carers (BD$\bar{X}$=7.200, AD$\bar{X}$=6.480, t(24)=-2.009, p<0.056), possibly explained by the smaller number of participants in this group. Standard deviations decreased slightly for the Early and Mid stages, but increased for the Late stage. Correlations were higher for the Early stage (.763) and for the Mid stage (.617), but low for the Late stage sample (.348), indicating more individual change than the means displayed in the Late stage.

Emotional support received rose significantly for the Early stage (BD$\bar{X}$=8.088, AD$\bar{X}$=9.265, t(33)=4.002, p<0.01), but not for the Mid stage, where a decrease in emotional support occurred. In the Late stage support increased between measurement points, but not significantly. Standard deviations increased for Early and Mid stages, indicating more heterogeneity between participants, but decreased for the Late stage. High correlation was revealed for the Early stage

(.840), Mid (.643) and Late (.612) stages, suggesting aggregate level change according to Krause (1999).

Tangible help received increased, but not quite in the significant range for Early stage participants (BD$\bar{X}$=4.824, AD$\bar{X}$=5.382, t(33)=2.014, p<0.052). Both Mid and Late stages also increased, but not significantly. Standard deviations increased for Early and Mid stages, but decreased for the Late stage participants. Correlations were .781 for Early, .620 for Mid and .581 for the Late stage.

Informational support increased markedly for all participants, in the significant range (EarlyBD$\bar{X}$=5.029, AD$\bar{X}$=6.206, t(33)=4.179, p<0.01; MidBD$\bar{X}$=5.548, AD$\bar{X}$=6.679, t(83)=4.724, p<0.01; LateBD$\bar{X}$=5.200, AD$\bar{X}$=7.040, t(24)=5.124, p<0.01). Standard deviations rose for all samples, and correlations were .675 for the Early sample, .564 for the Late sample, and only .219 for the Mid sample, indicating much movement in the rank order of participants between before and after measures for mid stage pwd and carers.

Tangible help provided decreased for all samples, but this change was only significant for Mid (BD$\bar{X}$=6.226, AD$\bar{X}$=5.595, t(83)=-2.578, p<0.05) and Late (BD$\bar{X}$=6.360, AD$\bar{X}$=5.080, t(24)=-2.718, p<0.05) stage participants. Standard deviations decreased slightly for Early and Late stages, but increased slightly for the Mid stage sample. Correlations were .759 for Early, .532 for Mid and .437 for Late stage samples.

Of great interest is the finding of significant loss of satisfaction for the Mid stage sample in the next three variables, while both Early and Late stages show stable means between before and after conditions.
Satisfaction with emotional support received (BD$\bar{X}$=0.800, AD$\bar{X}$=0.580, t(83)=-3.987, p<0.01), satisfaction with tangible help received (BD$\bar{X}$=0.800, AD$\bar{X}$=0.520, t(83)=-4.600, p<0.01) and satisfaction with information received (BD$\bar{X}$=0.740,

AD$\bar{X}$=0.610, t(83)=-2.472, p<0.05). All standard deviations for Early and Late stages samples are relatively stable, while the standard deviations for Mid stage are slightly rising. Correlations for Early are low, for Late they are very low for satisfaction with emotional and tangible help received and for Mid they are emotional .416, tangible .291 and informational .463.

Anticipated support for the Early group was significant (BD$\bar{X}$=8.353, AD$\bar{X}$=8.912, t(33)=2.409, p<0.05). Mid and Late expectations of support remained stable over both measures, and all standard deviations also remained stable. Correlations were high for the Early (.896), Mid (.739) and Late (.720) samples.

All other items in this grouping of samples did not show significant changes in means, standard deviations or unusually low or high correlations.

New Friends or No New Friends

Table 4 depicts the means, standard deviations and correlations related to change of social support in the group of carers of pwd who made new friends after the diagnosis of dementia (Newfriends) and carers who could not make new friends (Nofriends) groups.
The group of people who were able to make new friends (Newfriends) made up 53% (n=76) of the sample, and the group of people who could not make new friends (Nofriends) were 47% of the sample (n=67).

Contact with friends decreased significantly for both groups (NewfriendsBD$\bar{X}$=7.803, AD$\bar{X}$=6.197, t(75)=-6.610, p<0.01 and NofriendsBD$\bar{X}$=7.597, AD$\bar{X}$=5.970, t(66)=-7.814, p<0.01).
Standard deviations declined for the Newfriends sample, and were stable for the Nofriends sample. The correlation for the Newfriends sample was low, at .345, and was moderate (.528) for the Nofriends sample.

Contact with kin also decreased significantly for both samples, (NewfriendsBD$\bar{X}$=7.447, AD$\bar{X}$=6.447, t(75)=-5.235, p<0.01) (NofriendsBD$\bar{X}$=6.925, AD$\bar{X}$=6.254, t(66)=-3.847, p<0.01). Standard deviations were stable, and correlations for Newfriends were .612 and for Nofriends .616.

Tangible help received rose significantly for Newfriends (BD$\bar{X}$=5.197, AD$\bar{X}$=5.711, t(75)=2.123, p<0.05), and also increased for Nofriends, but not quite to a significant level. Standard deviations were stable for both samples. The correlations were high for Newfriends (.614) and for Nofriends (.694).

Informational support received also showed a significant increase in means for Newfriends (BD$\bar{X}$=5.487, AD$\bar{X}$=7.237, t(75)=7.184, p<0.01) and Nofriends (BD$\bar{X}$=5.224, AD$\bar{X}$=5.940, t(66)=3.372, p<0.01). Standard deviations were stable across both measures. The correlation for Newfriends was .437 and for Nofriends was .560.

Emotional support provided decreased for both samples, but was only significant for Nofriends (BD$\bar{X}$=10.224, AD$\bar{X}$=9.597, t(142)=-2.408, p<0.05). standard deviations were stable and the correlation for Newfriends was .576 and for Nofriends it was .702.

Tangible help provided reduced significantly for Newfriends (BD$\bar{X}$=6.211, AD$\bar{X}$=5.487, t(75)=-3.159, p<0.05) and for Nofriends (BD$\bar{X}$=6.313, AD$\bar{X}$=5.567, t(66)=-2.584, p<0.05). Standard deviations again were stable. The correlation for Newfriends was .645, for Nofriends .496.

Information provided increased for both groups, but only significantly for Newfriends (BD$\bar{X}$=.5.895, AD$\bar{X}$=6.473, t(75)=2.315, p<0.05). Standard deviations were stable. The correlation between measures for Newfriends was .473, while for Nofriends the correlation was .629.

Satisfaction with emotional support received decreased markedly for Newfriends (BD$\bar{X}$=.0800, AD$\bar{X}$=0.670, t(75)=-2.298, p<0.05), but there was little change for the Nofriends group. Standard deviations remained stable. Correlations were low, with .356 for Newfriends and .401 for Nofriends.

Satisfaction with tangible help received also decreased for both groups, but only significantly for the Newfriends group (BD$\bar{X}$=0.790, AD$\bar{X}$=0.620, t(75)=-2.706, p<0.05); Standard deviations rose slightly for the Newfriends and was more stable for the Nofriends. The correlation for the Newfriends was very low at .259, and also low for Nofriends at .384, indicating that individual change may have taken place which aggregate measures cannot account for.

Satisfaction with information received decreased again for both samples, but this time significantly for the Nofriends group (BD$\bar{X}$=0.780, AD$\bar{X}$=0.640, t(66)=-2.248, p<0.05), and was only close to significance for the Newfriends group. Standard deviations increased slightly for both samples. The correlation for Newfriends was extremely low at .177, indicating again that individual change may have occurred. The correlation for Nofriends was .420.

Negative interactions decreased slightly for people with new friends, but increased significantly for the Nofriends group (BD$\bar{X}$=6.642, AD$\bar{X}$=7.284, t(66)=2.724, p<0.05). Standard deviations were stable, but slightly higher in the Nofriends group. Correlations were .634 for the Newfriends sample, and .767 for the Nofriends sample.

All other items in this grouping of samples did not show significant changes in means, standard deviations or unusually low or high correlations.

Discussion

This study aimed to explore the change in social support for carers of people with dementia following the diagnosis of dementia. Comparisons were made between the change in social support of a sample of healthy older adults in America, over a 4 year period (Krause, 1999) and a group of carers of people with dementia (pwd) within Australia, after dementia was diagnosed. The hypothesis that carers of pwd would experience a greater loss of social support than the healthy older sample was supported. As expected, the change in social support was not uniform across measures.

Further comparisons were made in the present study between groups. Firstly, participants were divided into groups based upon type of dementia (Alzheimers, Cardiovascular and Other dementias). The hypothesis that the Other group would experience the greatest loss in social support was also confirmed.

Additionally, the social support of carers of pwd in different stages of dementia (early, mid and late) was compared. The hypothesis that the loss of social support was greatest at mid and late stages again was supported.

Finally, participants were grouped into those who made new friends to replace lost friends and those who did not make new friends. The prediction that who made new friends would have better social support than those who did not, was also upheld.

Comparisons between US healthy older population and Australian carers of pwd

In general, the direction of change was the same for the US and the Australian samples. That is, typically, both groups lost social support. However, for the sample of carers of pwd, the loss was far more extreme. For instance, the sample of carers of pwd had more contact with friends before diagnosis than the healthy older American sample. However, at the second measurement that changed dramatically. After diagnosis, the Australian sample of carers of pwd had lost approximately four times the social support than the American sample of healthy older adults.

The loss of kin shows a similar pattern as the loss of friends. Loss of kin seems to occur only about half as often as the loss of friends for both samples. The Australian sample of pwd and carers started off seeing more of their families than the American sample of healthy older adults, but after diagnosis the Australian sample of carers of pwd again experienced a loss approximately four times higher than the American sample of healthy older adults.

Therefore carers and pwd are losing friends and family, not just through natural causes, but also due to factors which are unique to conditions such as dementia. In the mid stage, pwd are losing the ability to function as a friend in a reciprocal relationship, as they could in the past. Friends are at a loss as how to interact in this situation, and after a couple of uneasy situations, might walk away. Carers, always near the pwd except for the occasions of respite, where they usually need to attend to daily life necessities, also lose many of their friends, as many of them will not accept the pwd. In this situation, the exclusion component of stigma comes to full realization, and the carer and the pwd are left isolated.

People will find reasons for staying away, by stating that they may not have been able to cope with one or another symptom of the illness, putting the blame on the victim of the illness, as one sentence overheard in a conversation between acquaintances of a pwd, e.g.

"The last straw was that she could not remember my name"

It appears that the inability to remember someone's name was interpreted as an insult, not the unfortunate symptom of memory loss in the advanced stages.

These findings indicate a severe loss of social support for carers and their pwd. Carers and their pwd are experiencing social isolation and related risks of lack of social stimulation through this exclusion. One such risk is depression, which may result from the devaluation and loneliness accompanying this cluster of problems, and also contributes to faster deterioration of the pwd.

Carers of pwd are also affected by the social isolation and associated depression while they are taking on the responsibility for a stigmatised person, and also may be put at risk of entering the latency period of 20-30 years when a person is still cognitively functioning, but experiences insufficient neural activity through lack of social contacts and the stimulating effects which radiate from social activities (Fratiglioni et al., 2000; Plattner & Erhardt, 2000; Valenzuela, 2006; Wilson, 2007).

Emotional, Tangible and Informational support received rose for both samples, mostly in the significant range. Although both samples lost social support on a significant level, both samples still seem to have a person or persons willing to listen to their problems. Some of this support might be provided by telephone, and, especially for carers for pwd, some might be given by the professionals, which carers of pwd are encountering. If people have made new friends in a carers group, some of their emotional comfort could come from conversations with people in similar situations.

Although family and friends are not staying in touch as they did before diagnosis of dementia, pwd and their carers are still receiving a slight increase in tangible support received and report a great increase in informational support. This phenomenon could be explained by government and community sponsored programs, such as dementia specific home help, monitoring and respite services, which also serve as centers for advice and educational programs for pwd and their carers. The Australian sample of carers of pwd gained around five times the informational support of the US sample, reflecting the great need for information in the very unsettling time of diagnosis and along the disease path.

In the present study, as in Krause's study, social support was assessed using a number of different measures. It was found that some measures of social support decreased significantly, some increased but not significantly, while others remained stable. The same was found in Krause's study, however, this was not always in the same measures.

For instance, Neal Krause (1999) proposed in his study that satisfaction with support received was the most stable measure of social support in the US sample of the general older population. The current study did not confirm these findings. Satisfaction with support was not the most stable measure of change in the Australian study, as Australian participants demonstrated not only loss in satisfaction levels across all measures of satisfaction, this sample experienced loss in satisfaction at a significant level in two of the four measures.

There was a significant decrease in satisfaction with emotional support in the Australian group of carers of pwd, whereas the US sample of healthy older adults only dropped insignificantly. Satisfaction with tangible support received also showed similar results. Since dissatisfaction is related to lowered quality of life and depression, this finding indicates that again the carers of pwd are at greater risk than a healthy older population, to develop depression and associated problems. Satisfaction with informational support did not change significantly for either group.

Negative interactions reduced for the US sample, but increased for the Australian sample near significance, a very disquieting and unexpected finding for the Australian carers of pwd. The finding that negative interactions increased for these participans seems very problematic, in the light of whatever little social support has remained, after so many friends and family are lost to the carer and pwd, part of this remaining social support is still is of poor quality, as negative interactions are very damaging to the people who experience them. Haley, LaMonde, Han, Burton and Schonwetter (2003) found, that the degree of impairment and symptoms of the pwd, or the duration of caregiving in years and the hours spent in caregiving per day, are not impacting as profoundly on the carer as ill health and negative interactions. Negative interactions are associated with higher levels of depression and lack of life satisfaction (Haley et al., 2003).

Negative interactions

There are a number of potential sources of negative interactions for carers of pwd. Friends sometimes don't understand the situation surrounding the carer and the pwd. Research on social support and unsupportive interactions and their association with depression among people with HIV found 11 types of unhelpful behaviours by people interacting with people with HIV. The following behaviours from this list are recognized as often occurring in interactions with pwd and their carers: A pessimistic attitude, criticism, patronizing, embarrassment or shame, avoidance of the person and insensitive actions or speech. Most carers and pwd have experienced these unhelpful behaviours, which are also related to stigma and depression (Ingram, Jones, Fass, Neidig & Song, 1999).

Family relations can be a source of negative interactions, for example by asking for help but not receiving any. Legal issues about property within families could also be the source of negative interactions, when the pwd might have behaviours which may impact on finances like giving money away to strangers or gambling. The details of any inheritance expected from family members could also be a point of disagreement, as these issues often are discussed at the time the pwd becomes unable to participate.

A rise in negative interactions could also relate to the lack of understanding in the general public about issues concerning dementia, embarrassment and shame experienced (Nolan, 2006) This could indicate that carers of pwd might also have problems with members of the wider community relating to the pwd's behaviour.

Antonucci et al. (2002) stated in their research about social relations, resource deficits and depressive symptomatology, that results consistently indicate that both resource deficits and negative social relations are directly and positively associated with depressive symptomatology (Antonucci, Lansford, Akiyama, Smith, Baltes, Takahashi, Fuhrer & Dartiques, 2002).

Eighty-five out of the143 survey participants sent letters or made explanatory comments on the survey pages. Some very relevant comments are presented here, to deliver the message of the participants in the participants' own words.

Alzheimers, Cardiovascular and Other types of dementia

In the current study, participants were grouped by type of diagnosis, resulting in three groups, i.e. Alzheimers (Alz), cardiovascular (Cardio) and other types of dementia (Other). While all three groups had dramatic reductions in friendships, the Other group reduced by the greatest amount. The Other group seemed to be homogenous in terms of the changes in social support. This larger reduction in friends may reflect the often more severe behavioural disturbances in people with Other types of dementia. As one of the carers in this group stated:

> *"Mother was a very social, outgoing and active person, loved family and always kept contact. She became very different overnight (vascular problems underlying frontal lobe damage). .."*

For both carers and pwd, the contact lost with friends and with kin is the type of contact which is the most stimulating, the face to face contact. People don't seem to come anymore, and visiting others has become cumbersome because of the difficulties of the pwd to get motivated. The problems with unusual and sometimes socially unacceptable behaviours are increasing towards the end of the early stage. Remote contact by telephone or letter is preserved a little better, but this type of contact is not as stimulating as seeing, touching and talking to people. Yet, there also appears to be some individual level change, where some carers actually experience much family support, although this group seems to be an exception rather than the rule.

This group is represented by comments such as the following:

> "...contact with family by phone, a little help and emotional support received from family, to a satisfactory level."
> "We seem to have plenty of family activities."
> "I am completely satisfied with the help of my own family has given my husbands and myself, however I can't say the same about my husband's sisters. They rarely come near us even though two live locally..."

In the item Informational Support, the groups Alz, Cardio and Other all showed a significant gain. In the Cardio group, the low correlation suggest that there may be individual level change in the data, and decreases in information for some people may offset increases in information for others, which is not captured in the aggregate analyses performed.

Emotional Support provided was only significantly lower for the Alzheimers group although participants in the Cardio group also had lower scores in the after diagnosis condition. Interestingly, participants in the Other group had increased scores in the after diagnosis condition, although not significant, indicating that this group is providing more emotional support now than before diagnosis. The group was very small in numbers (only 12 participants) and individual change was indicated at a high level, so experiences of participants seemed to be very diverse for the Other group. Comment:

> "She now has many different emotional expressions – close family and friends (are) very upset, and help each other a lot to understand."

The Alz and Cardio group provided significantly less tangible help to their friends and family, probably owing to the reduced face to face contact they are experiencing. Carers have problems with motivating their pwd to go out, so many opportunities of social encounters may be lost. Another factor might be the reduced financial circumstances most people find themselves in, restricting further the possibilities of helping someone else. The Other group also reduced provision of support, yet this group seems either too small to show significance or their particular circumstances did not allow them to help out with chores.

Another unexpected finding is, that satisfaction levels with emotional support and for tangible received support received fell significantly for Alz and Cardio. It could be explained by the overall outlook of the situation the carers of pwd find themselves in, with not much hope for change in the near future. Surprisingly, although satisfaction with tangible support also decreased for the Other group, but insignificantly (probably explained by the low number of participants in the group), satisfaction with emotional support was stable for this group. Although the information the groups received, sky rocketed for all groups, satisfaction with the information decreased for all, and for the Cardio group this change was significant. It seems, that the information provided to the carers of pwd might not always be what they wanted, or they might get more information than they asked for.

Negative interactions increased significantly for the Alz group. The Alz group is quite large with 102 participants. In contrast, the Other group is quite small (12participants), and although the difference in points was much larger for the Other group (-0.750), compared with the Alz group (-0.441), the analysis selected for this study did not find the difference significant. Since it could reasonably be expected, that negative interactions for the Other group would rise due to behavioural difficulties of the pwd, which is associated with this type of diagnosis, one could expect that negative interactions would have increased significantly for carers of pwd with a larger group of participants. The Cardio group was stable across measures.

Overall, the increase of negative interactions has very dire implications for the people who experience them, as described earlier.

Early, Mid and Late stages of dementia

As predicted in the present study, the early stage of dementia (Early) showed only a small decrease in social support relative to the Mid and Late stages, indicating that many friends were still coping with the changing situation at that point of the disease process. One carer said about her husband who was diagnosed about a year ago:

"(We) were overseas, husband (had) problems processing all the information, but all others also found (that there was) too much information. (Husband is) still presenting radio shows, (attends) Probus and Mah Jong, still drives..."

"Mother diagnosed with Alzheimers, now husband also diagnosed 6 months ago. Would like to spend more time with husband, before it is too late..."

In the mid stage (Mid), the picture changes dramatically. Contact with friends reduced by a full 2 points, indicating that the reciprocality of friendship was severely disturbed, to the point that many friends felt unable to cope and failed to return.

There are also some other co-existing conditions exacerbating the communication problems. Comment:

"As well as the dementia, poor to no hearing makes it hard to communicate with others."

In addition to communication problems, it is often difficult for the carer of pwd in the mid stage, to motivate the pwd to go out, as the pwd loses the ability to connect words to the experience of an outing.

The task for the carer to evoke interest by saying: "Let's go to Leura Gardens" only can be successfully completed if the pwd still can remember what the concept "Leura Gardens" means and can imagine how pleasant it might be to visit this beautiful garden. If the pwd can't remember what the concept means, the pwd needs to be very trusting of the carer and in an excellent mood to come on the outing without knowing where it leads. Very often the pwd will say "no", as "no" is always the safer option to avoid being caught out for not remembering once again.

Comments of carers:

> "Can't persuade my husband to go (on an outing or to visit)" and
> …"husband (is) quite unmotivated and needs "a lot of prodding" to do anything,"
> "Mother 90 years old diagnosed with Alzheimers, very unmotivated regarding previous activities and depending on daughter (60year old) for company."

In the late stage of dementia (Late), loss of friends was perceived more moderately by 1.6 points, as often in this stage the pwd needs to go into residential care, and the carer would regain more freedom. Many carers are visiting their pwd daily, usually at meal times, to assist with the meal and to spend time with their loved one. Comments:

> "Husband has entered nursing home – find that few staff understand Alzheirmers Disease…"
> "Mother (has) recently gone into full time professional care. I am a 'working carer' who was able to transfer her job to her mother's local area, thus was provided with 'social outlook' whilst caring for my mother at home."

Sometimes there also might be problems with nursing home admissions, due to disruptive behaviours, and the carer needs to persevere with the difficult situation until a solution has been found by services:

> "Husband cared for at home for 3 1/2 years, then abruptly placed in hospital – behaviours – nursing home can't take him"

The groups sorted by stage of dementia all showed a decrease in family support. As expected, the smallest loss in points was experienced by the Early group, the greatest loss in the Mid group, and a more moderate loss by the Late group. In the Early and Mid stages groups seemed more homogenous, but for Late stage there seemed more difference in experience, possibly explained by the changing circumstances for families who needed to admit their pwd to a nursing home.

> "…mother cared for at home, by son and daughter in law, until admission to nursing home for the last three years of her life. We were able to pay for help and respite when needed, to get breaks. Relatives were conspicuously absent for all this time, not even to pay a visit to mother, so were friends. I realize we were privileged to have the financial resources to have the breaks we needed and good staff in the aged care facility…"

Emotional support received rose significantly for the Early group, which is the stage when family and friends find out about the diagnosis and most people empathise with the pwd and the family. This is consistent with a rise in tangible support for this group. People providing emotional support might still be around to help out with chores.

At the Mid stage this empathy seems to run out, and a decrease in emotional support occurs. Friends and even family often cannot sustain emotional support, as many of them find it burdensome and would rather avoid the continuing scene of loss and grief. Comments:

"I do not want to talk about the problems because people will get bored."

In the Late stage social support increased, compared to the Mid stage, but not significantly. At this point in the disease process, the pwd might already be in a nursing home and life could be a little easier for the carer. Usually carers visit their pwd daily. Carer's lives are not anymore disrupted by the unusual sleeping patterns and nocturnal wanderings of their pwd, and the emergencies which occur in these situations. Some family and some friends might return and new friends may have become permanent.

Some families may have found their own solutions, often very original depending on cultural background. For example, one Middle Eastern family set up a house as a mini-nursing home, with widened door frames and hospital bed & equipment, to accommodate the father's needs. The father had Alzheimers disease, and his unmarried daughter lived with him for twenty years, doing exercises with him and caring for him until he passed away. Unfortunately, the unmarried daughter did not have much of a life in this situation. Again, the carer was isolated with the cared for.

Carers of pwd in the Mid stage group are not always able to take up the tangible help offered by community services they are entitled to, because sometimes the pwd, friends and family are in denial, and explain the diagnosis of dementia away by stating that forgetfulness is part of ageing, and the carer is exaggerating the deficiencies of the pwd. This occurs partly because of the stigma attached to dementia and the loss of status for the person and also because of the fear this diagnosis evokes. Yet, while others hide the condition or to explain it away, the carer will often be burdened excessively, as the pwd might reject any help from services offered by government and community. Comments:

"...I feel very scared of the future, as my person is in denial and has most of our friends convinced of this, too. He does not think he has a problem...so

> *help is not an option from friends...I am still working too many hours, so no time for social contacts."*
>
> *"Pwd will not admit to other than family that he has a problem. Therefore I have to be on hand to support him. He does not and would not accept that he needs a (professional) carer, other than me. Even the immediate family don't know the extent of his dementia..."*

Yet, in some situations this does not occur, and memory problems are openly accepted by all. Comment:

> *"My husband has Alzheimers, is 86 and physically well. I run a shop...and we live on the premises. Through customers and friends we get lots of support. (My husband) wanders in and out of the premises, walking the dog twice daily and trying to count backwards (in a complicated way) for brain exercise, having much difficulty."*

These huge differences in reports in the Mid stages of dementia explain the variations in statistical findings. Unfortunately, the latter scenario seems to be one of the lucky few, who take a practical approach and live quite happily with the condition.

Tangible help provided decreased for all three groups, Early, Mid and Late, but this change was only significant for Mid and Late stage participants. This is consistent with the impression, that carers of pwd in the mid and late stages seem the most exhausted carers and would not have the time or energy left to offer help to others.

Of great interest is the finding of significant loss of satisfaction for the Mid stage sample in all three satisfaction with support received variables, while both Early and Late stages show stable means between before and after conditions. This could be explained by the great strain this group is under. This low rating of satisfaction with emotional support received, tangible help received and information received, shows growing disillusionment with any support provided in the Mid stage of dementia, when the situation has already gone on for a long time, and the carer still cannot see an improvement of the situation ahead. Again, this can lead to depression and greater risk of illness in general for the carer.

Anticipated support for the Early group was significant – the only group which had a significant increase in this measure. This coincides with the rises in emotional and tangible help provided for this group, so carers of pwd at the early stage are still hoping that this increase in support will be ongoing. All other groups were stable.

New friends made or no friends made

The final comparison made in the present study was between those carers who made new friends to replace lost friends (Newfriends) and those who did not make new friends (Nofriends). The groups Newfriends and Nofriends were quite evenly divided in the sample. Typically, participants who made new friends did so by joining carers groups. Of the 67 people who could not join, 11 stated that there was no group, 30 stated that they did not have enough time, and 26 stated other reasons. Twenty-one people also stated why, how and/or where they joined groups, or why they did not continue attending groups. It was of interest to note that for both groups, contact with friends decreased significantly by about 1.600 points for both, indicating a similar experience for both groups.
Comments of Nofriends:

> "(I have) nothing in common with others in group, also do not drive, this restricts activities – have no car, have arthritis."
> "We have many old friends plus family, wife is one of ten children; no problems or difficult situations."

Contact with kin also decreased significantly for both groups sorted by new friends made or not. The loss was greater for the Newfriends group (I.000) than the Nofriends group (0.671). The greater loss of kin, combined with the great loss of friends for Newfriends could be part of the explanation why this group of people was making a greater effort to join up with carers groups

Tangible help received rose significantly for Newfriends and also increased for Nofriends, but not quite to a significant level. This may suggest that new friends might help each other a little when possible. People who joined carers groups and made new friends might have personalities that are more outgoing and easier to make friends.

Emotional support provided decreased significantly for Nofriends, but not for Newfriends, At the same time, information provided increased significantly for New Friends, but decreased for No Friends.
Both findings would support the assumption that participants in the Newfriends group are providing emotional and informational support to their new friends in the carers group.
Neither group has time to help others out with chores, so not surprisingly, tangible help provided reduced significantly for Newfriends and for Nofriends.

Negative interactions decreased slightly for people with new friends, but increased significantly for the Nofriends group, indicating that new friends may have balanced the scales towards more positive interactions regarding others. People who made no new friends may have less options to widen their skills regarding new and better ways of dealing with behaviours of their pwd, or to access information about services, debriefing of their situation and other important helpful social interactions encountered in a social group of likeminded people.

Satisfaction with tangible and emotional support received was reduced for both groups, but only significantly for New Friends. This might be because these participants could talk to their new friends in the carers group and establish that society is letting them down - a way of debriefing from their experiences and realising what should be done for them. The isolated group with no new friends may never even have considered that things could be better for them.

Implications for interventions

Further study could be undertaken to establish differences in the changes in social support for a sample of the general older population in Australia, to compare to the changes in social support for the population of pwd and carers in Australia, as well as to compare these changes to those experienced by the sample of healthy older Americans.
Further, it would be of interest to look at individual level change in a sample of carers of people with dementia. This could be achieved by using Kessler and Greenberg's Q^2 statistical method used by Krause (1999) to evaluate individual change. This is particularly important in light of the fact that the low correlations found in the present study, for some measures of social support, indicate that there is extensive individual change which is not captured by aggregate measures.

Another avenue of study which is worthwhile pursuing would be an investigation of the effects of other aspects of stigma associated with dementia. The present study was limited to an investigation of one aspect of stigma, social isolation. As such, the questionnaire used in this study was not aimed at investigating the problems of a group of people who live with a stigmatized condition, a questionnaire could be developed, which includes similar questions pertaining to stigma as the questionnaire used by Ingram et al. (1999).

The current study used the following questions regarding negative interactions, which could be asked of any other population, not afflicted by stigma: others making excessive demands, taking advantage, criticism and prying into the affairs of the carer of the pwd (Krause, 1999). It would be of great interest to develop a questionnaire which uses stigma related questions, similar to the questionnaire for people with HIV, used by Ingram et al. (1999), but modified for an older population living with the stigma of dementia.

Suggestions

The government needs to sponsor more programs, like some existing groups, which have developed over the years from very active carers and are still providing social events as barbecues, afternoon teas and dinners in nice places, on a monthly basis, to both carers and the pwd.

New groups need to be developed out of carer's groups, all over Australia, to access all carers and pwd who cannot travel very far, since many of them are losing licenses and resources necessary to keep a car in the family.

A network of buses needs to be made available, each with a driver who takes out a different group every day from a different vantage point, and a person to arrange and run worthwhile trips to many attractive and remarkable places around Australia, to get people out and about, and initiate the social contacts to make friends, social relations and stimulation so badly needed.

It is important, not only to provide respite, educate carers and the public and to form carer's support groups, but also to provide social programs that bring pwd and carers together in a non-threatening environment, and allow them to have rewarding and stimulating social experiences, to keep them as healthy as possible and make life worthwhile living again.

Limitations of the present study

There are a number of limitations inherent in the present study. Firstly, the small number of participants in particular groups, such as the Other types of dementia group, makes it difficult to draw firm conclusions.

A further limitation of the present study is that the before diagnosis social support measures were retrospective. Thus participants had to provide an indication of their social support, possibly many years previously. Particularly given the stressful nature of their lives as carers, it is possible that their recall of their social support prior to diagnosis is not entirely accurate. However, given the homogeneity of the sample in the present study, this issue did not appear to play a large role in the present study.

Krause (1999) indicates that the questionnaire used to assess social support is global and hence does not take into account the source of support. He cites this as a limitation in that it may be the case that some sources of support are declining, (for instance, support from a spouse), while others are improving (for instance, support from children). The present study is subject to this limitation to some degree, however, since many participants provided detailed statements indicating sources of support (some of which are included here), this serves to counteract this issue.

Conclusion

It seems that the direction of change in social support of carers of pwd after diagnosis is mostly comparable to that of healthy older adults. However, the change in the former group is of a far greater magnitude. Carers of pwd are experiencing a loss of social support four times as great than the healthy older population.

Although pwd and their carers are receiving a slight increase in emotional and tangible support and report a great increase in informational support, family and friends are not staying in touch as they did before the diagnosis of dementia, and most of the social contact seems to be by telephone rather than in face to face interaction, thus social stimulation is greatly decreased for carers and the pwd, and this part of the population could be described as socially isolated.

This is putting pwd at risk of faster deterioration and their carers at risk of slowly entering the same disease process, which begins with lack of stimulation and ends with a diagnosis of dementia (Wilson, 2007; Valenzuela, 2006; Plattner & Erhardt, 2000; Fratiglioni et al., 2000). As such, this study confirms that people with dementia and their carers are suffering the effects of stigma, in particular, the social isolation that results from being marginalised.

A very disturbing trend noted in this study was the slight, but important increase of negative interactions compared with the downtrend of negative interactions in the healthy older adults group. Negative interactions may offset and even outweigh positive social support (Krause, 1999), and are directly related to depression and reduced life satisfaction (Haley et al., 2003). Since depression is both a risk factor for dementia and other illnesses as well as a condition which can lead to faster deterioration of dementia, this trend is very worrying.

In summary, the carers of pwd have decreased quality of life and a great risk of depression, from social isolation, negative interactions and dissatisfaction with many aspects of their social lives. Thus, the stigma associated with dementia, which results, among other things, in social isolation, has a profound negative effect both on carers and people with dementia.

References:

Alzheimers Australia (2005). Dementia Estimates & Projections: Australian States & Territories, Access Economics (Eds.); www.alzheimers.org.au

Antonucci, T., Lansford, J., Akiyama, H., Smith, J., Baltes, M., Takahashi, K., Fuhrer, R. & Dartiques, J. (2002) Differences Between Men and Women in Social Relations, Resource Deficits, and Depressive Symptomatology During Later Life in Four Nations, *Journal of Social Issues 58*, 767-783

Australian Bureau of Statistics (2003). Disability, Ageing and Carers, Summary of Findings, 2003; www.abs.gov.au/AUSSTATS/abs@.nsf/Lookup

Australian Institute of Health and Welfare (AIHW) 2006. *Dementia in Australia: National data analysis and development.* AIHW cat. No. AGE 53. Canberra: AIHW

Bargh, J. A., Chaiken, S., Govender, R., & Pratto, F. (1992). The generality of the automatic attitude activation effect. *Journal of Personality and Social Psychology, 62*, 893-912.

Barrera, M., Jr. (1986). "Distinctions Between Social Support Concepts, Measures, and Models." *American Journal of Community Psychology 14*, 413-25.

Benbow, S. & Reynolds, D. (2000). Challenging the Stigma of Alzheimer's Disease. *Hospital Medicine, 61*, 174-177.

Brodaty, H. & Hadzi-Pavlovic, D. (1990). Psychosocial Effects on Carers of Living with Persons with Dementia, *Australian and New Zealand Journal of Psychiatry 24*, 351-361.

Brodaty, H. (1996) Caregivers and Behavioural Disturbances: Effects and interventions; *International Psychogeriatrics, 8*; International Psychogeriatric Association.

Butler, R. (1975) *Why survive: Old Age in America.* Baltimore, Md: Johns Hopkins University Press.

Butler, R. (2005). Looking back over my shoulder, *Ageism in the New Millennium,* Fall 2005.

Chen, M., & Bargh, J. A. (1997). Nonconscious behavioral confirmation processes: The self-fulfilling nature of automatically-activated stereotypes. *Journal of Experimental Social Psychology 33*, 541-560.

Cummings, J.L., & Benson, D.F. (2003). Dementia: A Clinical Approach (2nd ed), Boston: Butterworth Heinemann.

Dyck, P. (2006). Innovations in Care; *Partners in Care, 7*, 287–290; Lippincott Williams & Wilkins, Inc

Fratiglioni, L., Wang, H.X., Ericsson, K., Maytan, M., Winblad, B. (2000) Influence of social network on occurrence of dementia: a community based longitudinal study, *The Lancet, 355,* 1315-1319.

Goffman, E. (1963). *Stigma: Notes on the management of spoiled identity.* New Jersey: Prentice Hall.

Haley, W., LaMonde, L., Han, B., Burton, A., Schonwetter, R. (2003) Predictors of Depression and Life Satisfaction Among Spousal Caregivers in Hospice: Application of a Stress Process Model, Journal of Palliative Medicine 6, 215-224

Herskovits, E. & Mitteness, L. (1994) Transgressions and sickness in old age; *Journal of aging studies 8*, 327-340.

Hinton, L., Guo, Z., Hillygus, J., & Levkoff, S. (2000). Working with culture: A qualitative analysis of barriers to the recruitment of Chinese-American familiy caregivers for dementia research; *Journal of Cross-Cultural Gerontology* 15: 119-137; Kluwer Academic Publishers

Iliffe, S., De Lepeleire, J., Van Hout, H., Kenny, G., Lewis, A., Vernooij-Dassen, M. & The Diadem Group (2003). Understanding obstacles to the recognition of and response to dementia in different European countries: A modified focus group approach using multicultural, multi-disciplinary expert groups; *Aging & Mental Health;* 9, pp1-6.

Ingram, K., Jones, D., Fass, R., Neidig, J. & Song, Y. (1999). Social support and unsupportive social interactions: their association with depression among people living with HIV, *Aids Care 11,* 313-329

Jorm, A. (2001) History of depression as a risk factor for dementia: an updated review. *Australian and New Zealand Journal of Psychiatry;* 35, pp776-781

Kimble, D. (1992). *Aging of the Brain.* Biological Psychology (2nd ed.) Orlando FL: Harcourt Brace Jovanovich.

Krause, N. (1999). Assessing Change in Social Support During Later Life, *Research on Aging;* 21; 539, Accessed online 24th February 2008 www.sagepublications.com

Link, B., Cullen, F., Frank, J., Wozniak, J. F. (1987). The Social Rejection of Former Mental Patients: Understanding Why Labels Matter; *The American Journal of Sociology; 92,* 1461-1500

Link, B., & Phelan, J. (2001). Conceptualising Stigma. *Annual Review of Sociology 27, 363-385.*

Longino, C., (2005). The Future of Ageism: Baby Boomers at the Doorstep. *Generations 29,* 79-83

Mackenzie, J. (2006). Stigma and dementia: East European and South Asian family carers negotiating Stigma in the UK. *Dementia 5,* 233-247

Manthorpe, J., Iliffe, S. & Eden, A. (2004). Early Recognition of and Responses to Dementia: Health Professionals' Views of Social Services' Role and Performance. *British Journal of Social Work 34,* 335-348.

Nolan, L., McCarron, M., McCallion, P. & Murphy-Lawless, J. (2006). Perceptions of Stigma in Dementia: An Exploratory Study. *The School of Nursing and Midwifery, Trinity College Dublin.* The Alzheimer Society of Ireland

Palmore, E. (2005). Three Decades on Ageism. *Generations 29,* 87-90

Plattner, A., Ehrhardt, T., (2000). Social Networks and Dementia. *The Lancet, 356,* 433-434

Russell, R. (2001). In sickness and in health: A qualitative study of elderly men who care for wives with dementia. *Journal of Aging Studies, 15,* 351-367.

Sarkisian, C., Shunkwiler, S., Aguilar, I. Moore, A. (2006). Ethnic Differences in Expectations for Aging Among Older Adults; *JAGS 54, 1277-1282*

Saucier, M. (2004). Midlife and Beyond: Issues for Ageing Women; *Journal of Counseling and development 82,* 420-425

Schneider, J. (1988) Disability as a Moral Experience: Epilepsy and Self in Routine Relationships. *Journal of Social Issues, 44,* .63-78

Sutherland, R.J. & Rudy, J.W. (1989). Configural association theory: The role of the hippocampal formation in learning, memory and amnesia. *Psychobiology 17,* 129-144.

Truscott, M. (2003). Life in the Slow Lane, *Alzheimers Care Quarterly 4*, 11-17

Valenzuela, M.J. & Sachdev, P. (2003) Memory training alters hippocampal neurochemistry in healthy elderly. *Neuroreport 14,* 1333-1337

Wilson, R., Krueger, K., Arnold S., Schneider, J., Kelly, J., Barnes L., Tang, Y. & Bennett, D. (2007), Loneliness and Risk of Alzheimer's Disease, *Archives of General Psychiatry 64*, 234-40.

Appendix A

**Humanities and Social Sciences
Low Level Ethics Approval**

2 June 2008
Protocol No.00004

Dear Ms. Schwartz,

The School of Humanities and Social Sciences' ethics committee has met and reviewed your low level ethics approval application. After deliberation, the committee has deemed your application to be low risk and consequently approves your application.

Yours sincerely,

Daniel Cohen
School of Humanities and Social Sciences
Boorooma Street
Wagga Wagga NSW 2678
Email: dcohen@csu.edu.au

Appendix B

INFORMATION STATEMENT to POTENTIAL PARTICIPANTS

Dear Sir/Madam,
I am a student of psychology at Charles Sturt University in Bathurst and currently I am studying for my honours dissertation. Part of my research for this dissertation involves sending a questionnaire to the carers of people with dementia, and requesting carers to answer the questions.

The questions in this study are investigating social isolation of people with dementia and their carers – a problem I have come across frequently in my work with Alzheimers Australia NSW, and I feel passionately that our society needs to address this social issue.

The cut off day for return is Wednesday, the 30th July 2008 (last day to mail the questionnaire back).
We also included a self addressed & stamped envelope for the return of your completed questionnaire.
If you have any further questions, please ring Brigit Schwartz on 0410 391 800.

Below you will find the details of this research study:

The name of this study is:

Social Isolation Resulting from Stigma in Dementia

Investigators in this study are:
- Chief Investigator: Brigit Schwartz, student of psychology, psychology honours dissertation at Charles Sturt University, Bathurst, bschwartz@alznsw.asn.au
- Supervisor: Lauren Saling, lsaling@csu.edu.au

The host institution of this project is **Charles Sturt University, Bathurst.**

Benefits for Participants.

The benefit of the project for the participants is to alert the government of Australia through the Department of Health and Ageing, that there is a need in the community to facilitate social activities between pwd and their carers, by forming recreational groups. These groups have the capacity to enable pwd and carers to find new friends and social interactions within a group of people who have similar interests and circumstances and who feel comfortable with each other. Through these groups, the stimulation pwd and carers often have lost from their social support system, could be replaced. Social isolation, which puts people at risk of developing a dementing disease, and leads to faster deterioration of people who live with memory loss, could be prevented.

The community could benefit by the prevention of further cases of dementia in the future, and the costs involved in caring for pwd.

What you are asked to do.
Research participants are requested to fill in a questionnaire, asking questions about their social network before and after the person with dementia was diagnosed. This questionnaire tries to establish if the social network of the person with dementia AND the carer's social network have reduced through dementia. The time to fill in the questionnaire is estimated as approximately half an hour.

Risks involved.

The possible risks or side effects of filling in the questionnaire could be sadness and resentment of the attitudes, and lack of understanding of others, towards the situation the person with dementia and his or her carer find themselves in.

Counselling is available for research participants from the Helpline of Alzheimers Australia NSW, on 1800 100 500

What happens to the information collected?
Data collected will appear in literature published by Alzheimers Australia NSW and in a proposal to the Department of Health and Ageing. It is also intended to publish the literature in a journal about aged care.

Privacy.
To protect your privacy, the questionnaire is kept anonymous.
You do not have to participate in the project, and you can stop answering questions at any time.

➢ **NOTE:** The School of Humanities and Social Sciences Ethics Committee has approved this project. If you have any complaints or reservations about the ethical conduct of this project, you may contact the Committee through the Chair of the Committee:
➢ Dr. Daniel Cohen ➢ School of Humanities and Social Sciences ➢ Charles Sturt University ➢ Wagga Campus ➢ Boorooma Street, Wagga Wagga ➢ Tel: 6933 2565 ➢ Email: dcohen@csu.edu.au
➢ Any issues you raise will be treated in confidence and investigated fully and you will be informed of the outcome.

Appendix C

Table 1: Comparison between Neal Krause's older population in the US and people with dementia & their carers in Australia: Changes in Social Support Using Aggregate Descriptive Statistics

Dimensions of Support	US Data						Australian Data					
	Mean		Std deviation				Mean		Std deviation			
	Wave1	Wave2	Wave1	Wave2	correlation		Before	After	Before	After	correlation	
Contact w. friends	7.356	6.931	2.304	2.281	.406		7.706	6.091	1.902	1.682	.427	
Contact with kin	7.557	7.355	2.183	2.232	.461		7.203	6.357	1.774	1.782	.614	
Emotional received	10.409	10.825	3.699	3.514	.281		9.371	9.699	3.085	3.063	.671	
Tangible received	5.478	5.850	2.547	2.745	.441		5.308	5.713	2.353	2.451	.650	
Information received	4.977	5.228	2.105	2.262	.291		5.364	6.629	1.930	2.034	.485	
Emotional provided	10.553	10.324	3.332	3.283	3.53		10.280	9.895	2.713	2.860	.631	
Tangible provided	5.928	5.195	2.368	2.242	.489		6.259	5.525	2.319	2.391	.567	
Information provided	5.599	5.383	2.303	2.269	.327		5.860	6.063	1.977	2.117	.530	
Satisfaction with emotional received	.890	.886	.313	.318	.147		.790	.650	.409	.479	.414	
Satisfaction with tangible received	.916	.892	.278	.310	.079		.780	.590	.418	.493	.308	
Satisfaction with information received	.880	.889	.326	.315	.093		.740	.670	.439	.471	.470	
Satisfaction with support provided	.674	.676	.469	.468	.254		.760	7.10	.431	.454	.466	
Negative interaction	5.898	5.578	2.494	2.224	.392		6.650	6.902	2.633	2.799	.695	
Anticipated support	10.240	10.178	2.203	2.273	.382		8.664	8.776	2.632	2.563	.779	

The US sample varied in size between wave 1 and wave 2, range of participants 535 to 605, mean 584.142
In the Australian study 143 people participated in both conditions.

Comparison of social support in Alzheimers, Cardiovascular dementia and Other types of dementia

DIMENSIONS of SUPPORT	Alzheimers (N=102)					Cardiovascular (N=29)					Other (N=12)				
	Means		Std Deviations		Corr bef & after	Means		Std Deviations		Corr bef & after	Means		Std Deviations		Corr bef & after
	before	after	before	after		before	after	before	after		before	after	before	after	
CF	7.578	6.039	1.842	1.682	.485	8.103	6.620	1.896	1.761	.419	7.833	5.250	2.406	1.055	.090
CK	7.216	6.324	1.811	1.857	.636	7.138	6.517	1.505	1.765	.617	7.250!	6.250	2.179	1.138	.522
ER	9.284	9.480	3.173	3.111	.661	9.586	10.137	2.639	2.887	.687	9.583	10.500	3.528	3.060	.745
TR	5.422	5.716	2.357	2.479	.688	4.827	5.517	2.019	2.115	.323	5.500	6.167	3.060	3.070	.813
IR	5.352	6.363	1.958	1.850	.557	5.552	7.256	1.617	2.103	.122	5.000	7.333	2.449	2.902	.690
EP	10.206	9.745	2.585	2.820	.657	10.931	10.414	3.116	2.784	.625	9.333	9.917	2.605	3.450	.499
TP	6.196	5.529	2.329	2.332	.573	6.586	5.448	2.383	2.229	.567	6.000	5.667	2.174	3.339	.701
IP	5.813	5.990	2.018	2.169	.599	6.448	6.379	1.744	1.821	.282	4.833	5.917	1.801	2.429	.371
SER	0.780	0.670	0.413	0.474	.388	0.900	0.620	0.310	0.494	.435	0.580	0.580	0.515	0.515	.657
STR	0.760	0.630	0.426	0.486	.290	0.930	0.550	0.258	0.506	.302	0.500	0.420	0.522	0.515	.507
SIR	0.750	0.690	0.438	0.466	.429	0.860	0.690	0.351	0.471	.596	0.420	0.500	0.515	0.522	.507
SSP	0.760	0.740	0.426	0.443	.505	0.760	0.660	0.435	0.484	.269	0.670	0.670	0.492	0.492	.625
NI	6.657	7.098	2.550	2.916	.701	6.207	6.207	2.242	2.305	.551	7.667	6.917	3.916	2.811	.922
AS	8.578	8.677	2.623	2.580	.800	8.793	9.035	2.691	2.427	.646	9.083	9.000	2.745	2.892	.893

1010=significant difference

Comparison of social support in early, mid and late stage dementia

DIMENSIONS of SUPPORT	EARLY (N=34)					MID (N=84)					LATE (N=25)				
	Means		Std Deviations		Corr bef & after	Means		Std Deviations		Corr bef & after	Means		Std Deviations		Corr bef & after
	before	after	before	after		before	after	before	after		before	after	before	after	
CF	7.265	6.588	1.847	1.940	.775	7.857	5.857	1.896	1.538	.299	7.800	6.200	1.979	1.683	.500
CK	7.235	6.765	1.980	1.891	.763	7.190	6.155	1.846	1.739	.617	7.200	6.480	1.354	1.735	.348
ER	8.088	9.265	2.712	3.156	.840	9.798	9.714	3.041	3.145	.643	9.680	10.240	3.338	2.650	.612
TR	4.824	5.382	2.124	2.582	.781	5.571	5.941	2.366	2.495	.620	5.080	5.400	2.565	2.102	.581
IR	5.029	6.206	1.915	2.129	.675	5.548	6.679	1.954	2.007	.219	5.200	7.040	1.870	1.968	.564
EP	10.000	9.706	2.881	3.148	.822	10.214	9.988	2.565	2.818	.605	10.880	9.840	2.977	2.688	.445
TP	6.265	5.677	2.678	2.519	.759	6.226	5.595	2.192	2.425	.532	6.360	5.080	2.307	2.120	.437
IP	5.735	5.559	1.928	2.018	.810	5.976	6.262	1.963	2.129	.474	5.640	6.080	2.139	2.178	.382
SER	0.760	0.710	0.431	0.462	.555	0.800	0.580	0.404	0.496	.416	0.080	0.080	0.408	0.408	.250
STR	0.740	0.740	0.448	0.448	.547	0.800	0.520	0.404	0.502	.291	0.760	0.640	0.436	0.490	.164
SIR	0.790	0.790	0.410	0.410	.460	0.740	0.610	0.442	0.491	.463	0.680	0.720	0.476	0.458	.527
SSP	0.710	0.710	0.462	0.462	.433	0.790	0.710	0.413	0.454	.505	0.720	0.720	0.458	0.458	.405
NI	6.147	6.294	2.076	2.277	.830	6.833	7.298	2.866	2.973	.618	6.720	6.400	2.492	2.708	.894
AS	8.353	8.912	2.973	2.958	.896	8.714	8.714	2.482	2.452	.739	8.920	8.800	2.707	2.449	.720

1010=significant difference

	Comparison of social support with new friends made or not									
	New Friends (N=)					No Friends (N=67)				
	Means		Std Deviations		Corr before & after	Means		Std Deviations		Corr before & after
DIMENSIONS of SUPPORT	before	after	before	after		before	after	before	after	
CF	7.803	6.197	2.033	1.617	.345	7.597	5.970	1.750	1.758	.528
CK	7.447	6.447	1.865	1.914	.612	6.925	6.254	1.636	1.627	.616
ER	9.803	10.211	3.051	2.768	.586	8.881	9.119	3.072	3.292	.740
TR	5.197	5.711	2.406	2.393	.614	5.433 !	5.716	2.304	2.533	.694
IR	5.487	7.237	2.023	1.979	.437	5.224	5.940	1.824	1.882	.560
EP	10.329	10.158	2.826	2.833	.576	10.224	9.597	2.598	2.882	.702
TP	6.211	5.487	2.357	2.386	.645	6.313	5.567	2.292	2.414	.496
IP	5.895	6.473	2.082	2.163	.473	5.820	5.597	1.866	1.978	.629
SER	0.800	0.670	0.401	0.473	.356	0.750	0.630	0.438	0.487	.401
STR	0.790	0.620	0.410	0.489	.259	0.690 !	0.570	0.467	0.499	.384
SIR	0.800 !	0.700	0.401	0.462	.177	0.780	0.640	0.420	0.483	.420
SSP	0.760	0.740	0.428	0.443	.370	0.750	0.690	0.438	0.467	.057
NI	6.658	6.566	2.580	2.670	.634	6.642	7.284	2.712	2.912	.767
AS	8.645	8.855	2.611	2.415	.782	8.687	8.687	2.675	2.737	.779

!010=significant difference

Appendix D

Krause's (2000) Changes in Social Support Scale (modified for this study by Brigit Schwartz, 2008)

Preliminary Questions (Please, circle one option):

How long since the person with dementia (pwd) you are caring for has been diagnosed?

1year / 3years / 6years /10 years / over 10years

What stage of dementia is the pwd you are caring for in? (if in doubt, look at "stages of dementia" at the end of this questionnaire)

early stage / mid stage / late stage

What type of dementia has the pwd you are caring for been diagnosed with?

Alzheimers / Cardiovascular / Other

After diagnosis, have you been able to make new friends in a carer's group or other social activity?
yes   /   no

If yes, was this carer's group or social activity provided by a government organisation? yes / no

if no, please circle one option:

no group or activity available / no time to go out / other- please, describe:

After Diagnosis (NOW)	Before Diagnosis (PAST)
Contact with friends[a] 1. In the past two weeks, how often have you gone out to visit friends? not at all ■ once or twice ■ three to six times ■ more than six times ■ 2. In the past two weeks, how often have you had friends visit you? not at all ■ once or twice ■ three to six times ■ more than six times ■ 3. In the past two weeks, how often have you had contact by phone or letter with friends? not at all ■ once or twice ■ three to six times ■ more than six times ■ **Contact with kin**[a] 1. In the past two weeks, how often have you gone out to visit family? not at all ■ once or twice ■ three to six times ■ more than six times ■ 2. In the past two weeks, how often have you had family visit you? not at all ■ once or twice ■ three to six times ■ more than six times ■ 3. In the past two weeks, how often have you had contact by phone or letter with family? not at all ■ once or twice ■ three to six times ■ more than six times ■	**Contact with friends**[a] 1. Before diagnosis, within the space of two weeks, how often did you go out to visit friends? not at all ■ once or twice ■ three to six times ■ more than six times ■ 2. Before diagnosis, within the space of two weeks, how often did you have friends visit you? not at all ■ once or twice ■ three to six times ■ more than six times ■ 3. Before diagnosis, within the space of two weeks, how often did you have contact by phone or letter with friends? not at all ■ once or twice ■ three to six times ■ more than six times ■ **Contact with kin**[a] 1. Before diagnosis, within the space of two weeks, how often did you go out to visit family? not at all ■ once or twice ■ three to six times ■ more than six times ■ 2. Before diagnosis, within the space of two weeks, how often did you have family visit you? not at all ■ once or twice ■ three to six times ■ more than six times ■ 3. Before diagnosis, within the space of two weeks, how often did you have contact by phone or letter with family? not at all ■ once or twice ■ three to six times ■ more than six times ■

After Diagnosis (NOW)	Before Diagnosis (PAST)
Emotional support received from others[b]	**Emotional support received from others[b]**
1. Since diagnosis, how often has someone been right there with you (physically) in a stressful situation? never ■ once in a while ■ fairly often ■ very often ■	1. Before diagnosis, how often was someone right there with you (physically) in a stressful situation? never ■ once in a while ■ fairly often ■ very often ■
2. Since diagnosis, how often has someone comforted you by showing you physical affection? never ■ once in a while ■ fairly often ■ very often ■	2. Before diagnosis, how often did someone comfort you by showing you physical affection? never ■ once in a while ■ fairly often ■ very often ■
3. Since diagnosis, how often has someone listened to you talk about your private feelings? never ■ once in a while ■ fairly often ■ very often ■	3. Before diagnosis, how often has someone listened to you talk about your private feelings? never ■ once in a while ■ fairly often ■ very often ■
4. Since diagnosis, how often has someone expressed interest and concern in your well-being? never ■ once in a while ■ fairly often ■ very often ■	4. Before diagnosis, how often has someone expressed interest and concern in your well-being? never ■ once in a while ■ fairly often ■ very often ■
Tangible help received from others[b]	**Tangible help received from others[b]**
1. Since diagnosis, how often has someone provided you with some transportation? never ■ once in a while ■ fairly often ■ very often ■	1. Before diagnosis, how often did someone provide you with some transportation? never ■ once in a while ■ fairly often ■ very often ■
2. Since diagnosis, how often has someone pitched in to help you do something that needed to get done, like household chores or yard work? never ■ once in a while ■ fairly often ■ very often ■	2. Before diagnosis, how often did someone pitch in to help you do something that needed to get done, like household chores or yard work? never ■ once in a while ■ fairly often ■ very often ■
3. Since diagnosis, how often has someone helped you with shopping? never ■ once in a while ■ fairly often ■ very often ■	3. Before diagnosis, how often did someone help you with shopping? never ■ once in a while ■ fairly often ■ very often ■

After Diagnosis (NOW)	Before Diagnosis (PAST)
Informational support received from others[b]	**Informational support received from others**[b]
1. Since diagnosis, how often has someone suggested some action that you should take in order to deal with a problem you were having? never ■ once in a while ■ fairly often ■ very often ■	1. Before diagnosis, how often did someone suggest to you some action that you should take in order to deal with a problem you were having? never ■ once in a while ■ fairly often ■ very often ■
2. Since diagnosis, how often has someone given you information that made a difficult situation easier to understand? never ■ once in a while ■ fairly often ■ very often ■	2. Before diagnosis, how often did someone give you information that made a difficult situation easier to understand? never ■ once in a while ■ fairly often ■ very often ■
3. Since diagnosis, how often has someone told you what they did in a stressful situation that was similar to one you were experiencing? never ■ once in a while ■ fairly often ■ very often ■	3. Before diagnosis, how often did someone tell you what they did in a stressful situation that was similar to one you were experiencing? never ■ once in a while ■ fairly often ■ very often ■
Emotional support provided to others[b]	**Emotional support provided to others**[b]
1. Since diagnosis, how often have you comforted someone by showing them physical affection? never ■ once in a while ■ fairly often ■ very often ■	1. Before diagnosis, how often did you comfort someone by showing them physical affection? never ■ once in a while ■ fairly often ■ very often ■
2. Since diagnosis, how often have you listened to someone talk about their private feelings? never ■ once in a while ■ fairly often ■ very often ■	2. Before diagnosis, how often did you listen to someone talk about their private feelings? never ■ once in a while ■ fairly often ■ very often ■
3. Since diagnosis, how often have you expressed interest and concern in someone's well-being? never ■ once in a while ■ fairly often ■ very often ■	3. Before diagnosis, how often did you express interest and concern in someone's well-being? never ■ once in a while ■ fairly often ■ very often ■
4. Since diagnosis, how often have you been right there with someone (physically) who was experiencing a stressful situation? never ■ once in a while ■ fairly often ■ very often ■	4. Before diagnosis, how often were you right there with someone (physically) who was experiencing a stressful situation? never ■ once in a while ■ fairly often ■ very often ■

After Diagnosis (NOW)	Before Diagnosis (PAST)
Tangible help provided to others[b]	**Tangible help provided to others**[b]
1. Since diagnosis, how often have you provided someone with transportation? never ■ once in a while ■ fairly often ■ very often ■	1. Before diagnosis, how often did you provide someone with transportation? never ■ once in a while ■ fairly often ■ very often ■
2. Since diagnosis, how often have you pitched in to help someone do something that needed to get done, like household chores or yard work? never ■ once in a while ■ fairly often ■ very often ■	2. Before diagnosis, how often did you pitch in to help someone do something that needed to get done, like household chores or yard work? never ■ once in a while ■ fairly often ■ very often ■
3. Since diagnosis, how often have you helped someone with their shopping? never ■ once in a while ■ fairly often ■ very often ■	3. Before diagnosis, how often did you help someone with their shopping? never ■ once in a while ■ fairly often ■ very often ■
Informational support provided to others[b]	**Informational support provided to others**[b]
1. Since diagnosis, how often have you told someone what you did in a stressful situation that was similar to one they were experiencing? never ■ once in a while ■ fairly often ■ very often ■	1. Before diagnosis, how often did you tell someone what you did in a stressful situation that was similar to one they were experiencing? never ■ once in a while ■ fairly often ■ very often ■
2. Since diagnosis, how often have you suggested some action that someone should take in order to deal with a problem they were having? never ■ once in a while ■ fairly often ■ very often ■	2. Before diagnosis, how often did you suggest some action that someone should take in order to deal with a problem they were having? never ■ once in a while ■ fairly often ■ very often ■
3. Since diagnosis, how often have you given someone information that made a difficult situation clearer and easier to understand? never ■ once in a while ■ fairly often ■ very often ■	3. Before diagnosis, how often did you give someone information that made a difficult situation clearer and easier to understand? never ■ once in a while ■ fairly often ■ very often ■

After Diagnosis (NOW)	Before Diagnosis (PAST)
Satisfaction with support received from others[c]	**Satisfaction with support received from others**[c]
1. Since diagnosis, are you satisfied with the amount of emotional support that you have received from others, or do you wish that others would give you this kind of help more often or less often? satisfied ■ not satisfied ■	1. Before diagnosis, were you satisfied with the amount of emotional support that you received from others, or would you have wished that others had given you this kind of help more often or less often? satisfied ■ not satisfied ■
2. For the past few questions, we've been talking about things that people might have done for you or things they might have given to you. Thinking back over the past year, would you say you feel satisfied with this type of help, or do you wish it was given to you more often or less often? satisfied ■ not satisfied ■	2. For the past few questions, we've been talking about things that people might have done for you or things they might have given to you. Thinking back to before diagnosis, would you say you felt satisfied with this type of help in the past, or would you have wished it was given to you more often or less often? satisfied ■ not satisfied ■
3. The last questions were about the amount of information people may have given you to help you deal with the problems you might have had. Thinking back over the past year, would you say you feel satisfied with this type of help, or do you wish it was given to you more often or less often? satisfied ■ not satisfied ■	3. The last questions were about the amount of information people may have given you before diagnosis, to help you deal with problems you might have had then. Thinking back to before diagnosis, would you say you felt satisfied with this type of help in the past? Or would you have wanted more or less information? satisfied ■ not satisfied ■
Satisfaction with support provided to others[c]	**Satisfaction with support provided to others**[c]
The last questions were about things you may or may not have done for others. Thinking back over the past year, are you satisfied with the amount of help you've given to others, or do you wish you had helped others more often or less often? satisfied ■ not satisfied ■	The last questions were about things you may or may not have done for others. Thinking back over the past year, are you satisfied with the amount of help you've given to others, or do you wish you had helped others more often or less often? satisfied ■ not satisfied ■

After Diagnosis (NOW)	Before Diagnosis (PAST)
Negative interaction[b]	**Negative interaction**[b]
1. Since diagnosis, how often have you felt that others made too many demands on you? never ■ once in a while ■ fairly often ■ very often ■	1. Before diagnosis, how often did you feel that others made too many demands on you? never ■ once in a while ■ fairly often ■ very often ■
2. Since diagnosis, how often have you felt that others were critical of you and things you did? never ■ once in a while ■ fairly often ■ very often ■	2. Before diagnosis, how often did you feel that others were critical of you and things you did? never ■ once in a while ■ fairly often ■ very often ■
3. Since diagnosis, how often have you felt that those around you tried to pry into your personal affairs? never ■ once in a while ■ fairly often ■ very often ■	3. Before diagnosis, how often did you feel that those around you tried to pry into your personal affairs? never ■ once in a while ■ fairly often ■ very often ■
4. Since diagnosis, how often have you felt that others took advantage of you? never ■ once in a while ■ fairly often ■ very often ■	4. Before diagnosis, how often did you feel that others took advantage of you? never ■ once in a while ■ fairly often ■ very often ■
Anticipated support[d]	**Anticipated support**[d]
1. Since diagnosis, if you are sick in bed, how much can you count on the people around you to help out? not at all ■ a little ■ some ■ a great deal ■	1. Before diagnosis, if you were sick in bed, how much could you have counted on the people around you to help out? not at all ■ a little ■ some ■ a great deal ■
2. Since diagnosis, if you need to talk about your problems and private feelings, how much are the people around you willing to listen? not at all ■ a little ■ some ■ a great deal ■	2. Before diagnosis, if you needed to talk about your problems and private feelings, how much would the people around you have been willing to listen? not at all ■ a little ■ some ■ a great deal ■
3. Since diagnosis, if you need to know where to go to get help with a problem you are having, how much are the people around you willing to help out? not at all ■ a little ■ some ■ a great deal ■	3. Before diagnosis, if you needed to know where to go to get help with a problem you were having, how much would the people around you have been willing to help out? not at all ■ a little ■ some ■ a great deal ■

Stages of cognitive decline:

The website of the American Alzheimers Association's National Office in Chicago has provided the following guidelines to establish concepts of mild, moderate, moderately severe and severe Alzheimer's disease.

Experts have documented common patterns of symptom progression that occur in many individuals with Alzheimer's disease and developed several methods of "staging" based on these patterns.

Staging systems provide useful frames of reference for understanding how the disease may unfold and for making future plans. But it is important to note that not everyone will experience the same symptoms or progress at the same rate. People with Alzheimer's die an average of four to six years after diagnosis, but the duration of the disease can vary from three to 20 years.

The framework for this section is a system that outlines key symptoms characterizing seven stages ranging from unimpaired function to very severe cognitive decline. This framework is based on a system developed by Barry Reisberg, M.D., Clinical Director of the New York University School of Medicine's Silberstein Aging and Dementia Research Center.

Within this framework, we have noted which stages correspond to the widely used concepts of mild, moderate, moderately severe and severe Alzheimer's disease. We have also noted which stages fall within the more general divisions of early-stage, mid-stage and late-stage categories.

Note by researcher: please, use the scale for Alzheimer's disease for other forms of dementia, simply to establish where approximately the person with dementia you are caring for might fit in, regarding the severity of the condition.

Stage 1:

No impairment (normal function)

Unimpaired individuals experience no memory problems and none are evident to a health care professional during a medical interview.

Stage 2:

Very mild cognitive decline (may be normal age-related changes or earliest signs of Alzheimer's disease)

Individuals may feel as if they have memory lapses, especially in forgetting familiar words or names or the location of keys, eyeglasses or other everyday objects. But these problems are not evident during a medical examination or apparent to friends, family or co-workers.

Stage 3:

Mild cognitive decline
Early-stage Alzheimer's can be diagnosed in some, but not all, individuals with these symptoms

Friends, family or co-workers begin to notice deficiencies. Problems with memory or concentration may be measurable in clinical testing or discernible during a detailed medical interview. Common difficulties include:

- Word- or name-finding problems noticeable to family or close associates
- Decreased ability to remember names when introduced to new people
- Performance issues in social or work settings noticeable to family, friends or co-workers
- Reading a passage and retaining little material
- Losing or misplacing a valuable object

Decline in ability to plan or organize

Stage 4:

**Moderate cognitive decline
(Mild or early-stage Alzheimer's disease)**

At this stage, a careful medical interview detects clear-cut deficiencies in the following areas:

- Decreased knowledge of recent occasions or current events
- Impaired ability to perform challenging mental arithmetic-for example, to count backward from 75 by 7s

Decreased capacity to perform complex tasks, such as planning

- dinner for guests, paying bills and managing finances
- Reduced memory of personal history

The affected individual may seem subdued and withdrawn, especially in socially or mentally challenging situations

Stage 5:

**Moderately severe cognitive decline
(Moderate or mid-stage Alzheimer's disease)**

Major gaps in memory and deficits in cognitive function emerge. Some assistance with day-to-day activities becomes essential. At this stage, individuals may:

- Be unable during a medical interview to recall such important details as their current address, their telephone number or the name of the college or high school from which they graduated
- Become confused about where they are or about the date, day of the week or season

- Have trouble with less challenging mental arithmetic; for example, counting backward from 40 by 4s or from 20 by 2s
- Need help choosing proper clothing for the season or the occasion
- Usually retain substantial knowledge about themselves and know their own name and the names of their spouse or children

Usually require no assistance with eating or using the toilet

Stage 6:

Severe cognitive decline
(Moderately severe or mid-stage Alzheimer's disease)

Memory difficulties continue to worsen, significant personality changes may emerge and affected individuals need extensive help with customary daily activities. At this stage, individuals may:

- Lose most awareness of recent experiences and events as well as of their surroundings
- Recollect their personal history imperfectly, although they generally recall their own name
- Occasionally forget the name of their spouse or primary caregiver but generally can distinguish familiar from unfamiliar faces
- Need help getting dressed properly; without supervision, may make such errors as putting pajamas over daytime clothes or shoes on wrong feet
- Experience disruption of their normal sleep/waking cycle
- Need help with handling details of toileting (flushing toilet, wiping and disposing of tissue properly)
- Have increasing episodes of urinary or fecal incontinence
- Experience significant personality changes and behavioral symptoms, including suspiciousness and delusions (for example, believing that their caregiver is an impostor); hallucinations (seeing or hearing things that are not really there); or compulsive, repetitive behaviors such as hand-wringing or tissue shredding

Tend to wander and become lost

Stage 7:

**Very severe cognitive decline
(Severe or late-stage Alzheimer's disease)**

This is the final stage of the disease when individuals lose the ability to respond to their environment, the ability to speak and, ultimately, the ability to control movement.

- Frequently individuals lose their capacity for recognizable speech, although words or phrases may occasionally be uttered
- Individuals need help with eating and toileting and there is general incontinence of urine

Individuals lose the ability to walk without assistance, then the ability to sit without support, the ability to smile, and the ability to hold their head up. Reflexes become abnormal and muscles grow rigid. Swallowing is impaired.

Alzheimer's Association National Office 225 N. Michigan Ave., Fl. 17, Chicago, IL 60601 © 2008 Alzheimer's Association.
All rights reserved.
http://www.alz.org/alzheimers_disease_stages_of_alzheimers.asp

Scientific Publishing House
offers
free of charge publication
of current academic research papers, Bachelor´s Theses, Master's Theses, Dissertations or Scientific Monographs

If you have written a thesis which satisfies high content as well as formal demands, and you are interested in a remunerated publication of your work, please send an e-mail with some initial information about yourself and your work to *info@vdm-publishing-house.com*.

Our editorial office will get in touch with you shortly.

VDM Publishing House Ltd.
Meldrum Court 17.
Beau Bassin
Mauritius
www.vdm-publishing-house.com

Druck: KN Digital Printforce GmbH · Schockenriedstraße 37 · 70565 Stuttgart